Also by John Sutherland

Is Heathcliff a Murderer?
Can Jane Eyre Be Happy?
Who Is Dracula's Father?
The Brontësaurus

FRANKENSTEIN'S
BRAIN

**Puzzles and Conundrums in Mary
Shelley's Monstrous Masterpiece**

JOHN SUTHERLAND

ICON

Published in the UK in 2018
by Icon Books Ltd, Omnibus Business Centre,
39–41 North Road, London N7 9DP
email: info@iconbooks.com
www.iconbooks.com

Sold in the UK, Europe and Asia
by Faber & Faber Ltd, Bloomsbury House,
74–77 Great Russell Street,
London WC1B 3DA or their agents

Distributed in the UK, Europe and Asia
by Grantham Book Services,
Trent Road, Grantham NG31 7XQ

Distributed in the USA
by Publishers Group West,
1700 Fourth Street, Berkeley, CA 94710

Distributed in Australia and New Zealand
by Allen & Unwin Pty Ltd,
PO Box 8500, 83 Alexander Street,
Crows Nest, NSW 2065

Distributed in South Africa
by Jonathan Ball, Office B4, The District,
41 Sir Lowry Road, Woodstock 7925

Distributed in India by Penguin Books India,
7th Floor, Infinity Tower – C, DLF Cyber City,
Gurgaon 122002, Haryana

Distributed in Canada by Publishers Group Canada,
76 Stafford Street, Unit 300
Toronto, Ontario M6J 2S1

ISBN: 978-178578-408-8

Typeset in Photina MT by Marie Doherty

Printed and bound in Great Britain
by Clays Ltd, Elcograf S.p.A.

Contents

III. AFTERTHOUGHTS

Preface

Being puzzled by great works of literature is, I've always believed, a healthy response. Solving conundrums, as best they can be solved, makes reading pleasurable (a reward which is not always high on the agenda in the universities I have worked in).

I have, over the years, written several books of this enjoyably querulous kind. Of this latest I will say that *Frankenstein* is brain-rackingly puzzling. I have done my best to think my way through the narrative obstacles Mary Shelley throws up – sometimes, surely, to tease the reader. But being teased too can be enjoyable.

Choice of text

There are several usable texts of *Frankenstein*, ranging from facsimiles of the manuscript copy-text (with Percy Shelley's editorial revision), to the first three-volume edition (with Percy Shelley as midwife) published in 1818, to the 1823 theatre tie-in text (with William Godwin as midwife),* to the 1831 Standard Novel edition (with Mary Shelley, at last, delivering

....

* Produced after Godwin and his daughter saw Richard Brinsley Peake's long-running dramatic adaptation, entitled *Presumption*, in London in July 1823. The theatrical production did much to popularise the novel after the three-volume initial edition failed even to sell out its 500 copies.

her own book in her own person, with an invaluable explanatory preface), to an eclectic assortment of modern editions.

The 1831 text, the last corrected in Mary Shelley's lifetime (and with no interfering hands), is a tempting choice. But much had happened in her life – almost all of it catastrophic – since 1816 when Mary Godwin awoke with her primal dream-version of the story. The vibrant 'young girl' (as she called herself, looking back in 1831) was now a depressed widow and hard-pressed single mother. A submissive religiosity and fatalism in 1831 runs against the grain of the original free-thinking creation of 1818. A sharp edge has been blunted.*

Used in what follows is the 1818 text, it being, of the printed versions, closest to what was fresh in Mary Godwin's mind in summer 1816, by Lake Geneva. I am an admirer of Gutenberg.org which has made a huge library of 19th-century fiction freely available. I have used the 1818 Gutenberg text (reproduced faithfully from the 1818 three-volume edition). Quotations can be found in seconds by the Gutenberg text's word search facility.

Would that some sorcery could call up the dream which Mary tells us was the blueprint for the novel. Or that the script she used when reading out her (then) hour-long tale to the company at Villa Diodati had survived. Or that there were some Boswell record of the conversations she and her husband had about how to turn her primal 'idea' into something

* Marilyn Butler's 1998 Oxford World's Classics edition usefully lists the changes between 1818 and 1831.

publishable. Or what Byron's and his doctor friend John Polidori's suggestions were after they heard her narration.

Whatever these regrets, the reader should bear in mind that the novel began as a vocal performance – *recitative* – in Villa Diodati to a supremely gifted group of literary people. Some of that survives in every version of *Frankenstein*, if only as the distant echo of a young girl's voice.

In the above paragraphs I have referred to her as both Mary Godwin and Mary Shelley. She was Miss Godwin when, aged eighteen, she first conceived *Frankenstein* and Mrs Shelley when the 1818 edition came out, having married Percy (by whom she had had two illegitimate children) on 30 December 1816. She was the widowed Mrs Percy Shelley when the 1823 and 1831 editions came out. All that she had then of her drowned husband was his heart, in a silk pouch, pressed next to hers.* And memories.†

Recent criticism and biography mark a significant feminist strand in her makeup with the name 'Mary Wollstonecraft Godwin' or 'Mary Wollstonecraft Shelley', according to date. To unclutter this short book I use 'Mary' where it seems right. Anne K. Mellor, a critic I am indebted to, warns of the possible condescension in a male commentator's using women's forenames. I have tried to balance that by plentiful use of 'Victor' and 'Percy'. Somehow I can't bring myself to call Byron 'George'.

And what to call the humanoid at the centre of the story?

....

* See page 127.

† A brief biography of Mary Shelley can be found on page 14.

'He' (although his later behaviour is that of an 'It') I call 'Creature' other than on occasions when he becomes wholly a 'Monster'. The novel isn't consistent.*

The opening section of this book will look in more detail at the background to and composition of the novel, briefly touched on above, and the life of Mary Shelley.

In the central section beginning on page 33 the entries follow, in rough sequence, the chain of narrative: from the retrospect opening in the Arctic, looping back to Victor Frankenstein's family upbringing in Geneva, his going to university in Ingolstadt, his discoveries and fateful experiment; the mysteries surrounding the creation of the Creature; the mistreatment which makes the Creature monstrous; his crimes and vengeance against his maker and society; Frankenstein's pursuit of the thing he has made to the ends of the earth; and finally their deaths, a kind of Liebestod, in the icy wasteland and waters of the North Pole. (A summary of the narrative can be found on page 51.)

After this there ensues a series of 'afterthoughts' on such subjects as Frankenstein in film and popular culture, Percy's likely contribution, and what Mary earned from the book – plus, as an appendix, a retelling of *Frankenstein* by John Crace, in his own inimitable 'digest' style.

Because I anticipate that this is a book which will be dipped into I occasionally quote more than once relevant passages which any beginning-to-end reader is advised to skip.

....

* See the entry on what to call him, if anything other than a row of dashes, below, page 83.

I.
BACKGROUND AND
COMPOSITION

Rain, rain go away

⤞⤝

Three novels, 'three-deckers' all of them,* have lived on to our time from 1818, growing in reputation with the passing of two centuries: *Frankenstein*, published anonymously (on 1 January that year); *Persuasion*, by Jane Austen (published under her own name, posthumously, in January); and *The Heart of Midlothian* by Walter Scott (published under pseudonym in July).

One hesitates as to whether to include Thomas Love Peacock's satire on Shelley's set and their Romantic nonsense (as Peacock saw it), *Nightmare Abbey* (November 1818). Or *Northanger Abbey* (published alongside *Persuasion*), a satire on gothic fiction, the abbey-loving genre to which *Frankenstein* loosely belongs.

Enough to say there are many *anni mirabiles* in English literature; 1818 is among them. And of particular interest is the way in which the above novels of the year seem at times to be conversing with each other.

Scott furthered the conversation by reviewing *Frankenstein*. 'Peculiar', was the Wizard of the North's verdict. It was, we apprehend, like nothing he had read before. And nothing like

....
* That is, published in three volumes, to meet the demands of the circulating library system of the time.

Scott. He struggled, somewhat, to define what it was. Idea-rich gothic, one might call it. Ideas and gothic rarely run in tandem.

Jane Austen died six months before *Frankenstein* was published. Had she lived to read it she might have written a spoof to rival Mrs Radcliffe's spine-tinglers (spectacularly idea-poor gothic novels) in *Northanger Abbey*.

We, like Scott, have become, over the past 200 years, fascinated by the peculiarity of Mary Shelley's novel and the ideas driving it. Most peculiar perhaps is its being a work that owes its existence to rain.

The foul weather originated, far away, in Indonesia, with the eruption of Mount Tambora. It hit seven on the Volcanic Explosivity Index, making it the largest such eruption in a thousand years – a near extinction-level event:

> Sixty-mega-tons of sulfur were shot forty-three kilometers into the stratosphere within the space of a few hours ... blocking sunlight and lowering Earth's surface temperature by several degrees. The slight decrease in temperature was especially devastating because it occurred at a time when Earth's temperature was already cooler due to the Little Ice Age.*

In Switzerland and Germany's mountainous regions, where the Shelleys were vacationing with Lord Byron, it was

---

* Abigail Heiniger, 'Ragnok in Mary Shelley's *Frankenstein*: The Revenge of the Hrimthursar', *The Journal of Ecocriticism*, Vol. 3, No. 1 (2011), https://ojs .unbc.ca/index.php/joe/article/view/234 end-of-the-world weather. Crops failed. Britain had grain reserves to see it through 1815–17. Mainland Europe was, in places, less prudent – especially those regions with large peasant populations and poor agriculture.

As Mary and the others were composing ghost stories in the Villa Diodati by Lake Geneva there were starving peasants in the hills of Northern Europe scavenging in the incessant gloom and downpour for roots and scant summer berries for the coming winter. Lenten fare. Mary must have witnessed or heard about such hardship. The Creature she invented lives sparsely on tubers and berries and resides by preference on icy hills where he is, unlike humankind, immune to cold, rain and the pangs of hunger. Less, at times, a superman than a super peasant.

Bad weather, from the wet 'dreary' night on which the Creature comes into the world to the year-long Arctic ice where he and Victor elect to leave the world, is the climatic norm in *Frankenstein*. One turns the mental central heating up reading the novel.

It was not merely rain, chills, and dark clouds with dark linings. 1816 saw storms the like of which could not be recalled in living memory. As a child Victor is literally thunderstruck by the cataclysmic storm he witnesses whose fearsome electrical discharge reduces 'an old and beautiful oak' to 'ribbands of wood ... utterly destroyed' (the word 'ribbands' – ribbons – catches, momentarily, the female voice. The male voice would have said 'splinters').

The mood of *Frankenstein*, its internal climate, is nervous, depressive, verging at moments on suicidally gloomy. The Creature kills himself. Suicide was everywhere in 1815–17; Mary – the daughter of a mother who made serious attempts at self-destruction* – vibrated to it, like a tuning fork. On 9 October 1816, Mary's stepsister Fanny, aged 22, killed herself in a lodging house with an overdose of laudanum. Her father refused to identify the body and she was buried in a pauper's grave. On 10 December, the body of Percy Shelley's abandoned wife Harriet, aged 21, in a condition of advanced pregnancy (by another man), was found in London's Serpentine.† Suicide is assumed.

These miserable tragedies occurred while Mary Shelley was getting the manuscript of *Frankenstein* in shape for publication. What, she must have wondered, if she were to suffer the same fate as her predecessor in Percy's marital bed? She and Percy married days after he was liberated to do so by Harriet's self-destruction. He wanted to wait a decent interval before taking a new wife. She (now pregnant herself) threatened suicide if he did not release her from humiliating concubinage.

In short, 1816 could be seen as a harbinger of apocalypse. It was the 'year without a summer', otherwise called 'the poverty year', and resulted in a (less deadly) eruption of gothic

* She may have fantasised that her mother's death (in fact from puerperal fever), eleven days after Mary's birth, was a kind of self-destruction.

† For the complicated circumstances of Harriet's death see John Lauritsen, http://paganpressbooks.com/jpl/HS-WIFE.HTM

fiction in Villa Diodati, at Coligny, alongside Lake Geneva, where the English tourists were staying.* Rarely has a rainy holiday been so productive for literature.

Pent up by the foul weather, which clouded even the magnificent Alps and lakes beneath them, Byron, who had taken the lease on the Villa Diodati, proposed that the company – himself, Percy and Mary (both of whom he had only recently met), Claire Clairmont (Mary's stepsister and Byron's mistress), and Byron's companion physician, John Polidori – beguile the rainy days and nights with a competition to come up with the most spine-chilling ghost story their bored, brilliant minds could invent. Something to rival the German *Schauerroman* ('shudder novel').

A sample volume of short stories (translated into French), *Fantasmagoriana*, was circulating among the company. Surely they could come up with something better? It would be fiction as sport. And an escape from the apocalypse outside, while they got to know each other better. In more than one sense: Claire, although she may not have known it, was pregnant by Byron; Mary became pregnant at the Villa; John Polidori may have had something more than a physician's relationship with the bisexual Byron.

....

* It is at Coligny, in the cottage alongside the villa where Shelley, Mary and Claire were staying, that Victor Frankenstein intends to live with his wife, Elizabeth. The Creature puts an end to that happy prospect. For a description and pictures of the villa see https://www.rc.umd.edu/reference/misc/shelleysites/tours/tour1816.html

Mary was struck by the legend that Milton had once, like them, resided in the Villa Diodati. She elected to rewrite *Paradise Lost* as *Frankenstein*, later blazoning the fact with quotation on the title page for any reader too slow to catch on.

Claire Clairmont was outclassed and fell by the wayside. Shelley and Byron started to play but soon fizzled out: literature was, in the final analysis, more than a parlour game for them. None the less, as a striking entry in Polidori's diary, for 18 June, testifies, everyone remained keen listeners. At midnight, the witching hour, the talk turned truly 'ghostly':

> L[ord] B[yron] repeated some verses of Coleridge's Christabel, of the witch's breast; when silence ensued, and Shelley, suddenly shrieking and putting his hands to his head, ran out of the room with a candle. Threw water on his face, and after gave him ether. He was looking at Mrs. S[helley], and suddenly thought of a woman he had heard of who had eyes instead of nipples, which, taking hold of his mind, horrified him.*

One recalls how prone Victor Frankenstein is to recoil and faint at moments of stress in the novel. Rarely has a hero been more in need of the phial of smelling salts in his waistcoat pocket – e.g.:

....

* It has been suggested that, in addition to Coleridge, Shelley, whose mind was a vibrant literary echo-chamber, had subconsciously recalled the line in Shakespeare's *Henry VI*, 'At their mother's moist'ned eyes babes shall suck'. Mothers and motherlessness are a major theme in *Frankenstein*.

I was troubled: a mist came over my eyes, and I felt a faintness seize me; but I was quickly restored by the cold gale of the mountains. I perceived, as the shape came nearer, (sight tremendous and abhorred!) that it was the wretch whom I had created.

You could, as they say, have knocked him over with a feather. There is a point at which Romantic hypersensitivity merges into the wimp. There are many such, exclamation-mark rich, moments in the novel. And one may also note that one of Percy's nicknames was 'Victor'.

The relevant lines in *Christabel* which threw Percy into fits are:

> Then drawing in her breath aloud,
> Like one that shuddered, she unbound
> The cincture from beneath her breast:
> Her silken robe and inner vest
> Dropped to her feet, and full in view
> Behold! her bosom and half her side,
> Hideous, deformed, and pale of hue –
> A sight to dream of, not to tell!
> And she is to sleep by Christabel!

'Nightmare Abbey' (à la Peacock's satire) would have been an apt name for Villa Diodati, June 1818. A friend of Shelley, less than friendly with Byron, and amused immensely by Coleridge ('Mr Flosky', who sprinkles salt on candles to turn them blue and generate nightmares at noon), Peacock poked fun in his novel at the coterie who, as he cannot have known, were spinning their nightmares at exactly the same time.

Polidori stayed on message and after a false start concerning a skull-headed woman (a Medusa without snakes), charged up his imagination to produce 'The Vampyre'. The idea was suggested by Byron, and the monster Polidori came up with is recognisably a cartoon of the mad, bad and dangerous to know lord. Dangerous to Polidori, it turned out: annoyed by the story, Byron got rid of his physician shortly after.

Why, one asks, does *Frankenstein* matter two centuries later? We may note that, despite the valiant efforts of critics, none of Mary's other six novels has had overwhelming appeal for posterity. Everyone – whether they've read it or not – 'knows' *Frankenstein*. How many know *Mathilda?**

Partly *Frankenstein* endures because of the glamour (a word which Walter Scott reminds us means 'magic') of the circumstances in which it was devised, and more so because, as Brian Aldiss, the dean of British science fiction, has plausibly argued, *Frankenstein* is foundational to his genre.[†] Mary Shelley's novel foresees an anthropocene future (as we now call it): humankind, with science in one hand and

---

* A self-revealing novel, uncovering layers of paternal incest, suicide and despair which commentators see as part of Mary Wollstonecraft Shelley's make-up.

[†] See Aldiss's history of sci-fi, *Trillion Year Spree* (2001), and his novel, *Prometheus Unbound* (1973).

technology in the other can play God. It invariably turns out more problematic than utopianists (such as Percy Shelley) have predicted. *Frankenstein* is more topical today than it was in 1818.

Aldiss puts his case for Mary Shelley dogmatically:

> But the use of [her] modernised Faust theme is particularly suited to **the first real novel of science fiction**: Frankenstein is *the* modern theme, touching not only science but man's dual nature, whose inherited ape curiosity has brought him both success and misery. His great discovery apart, Frankenstein is a meddler and victim, staggering through a world where heavenly virtues are few (though the fiend *reads* of them). Instead of hope and forgiveness, there remain only the misunderstanding of men and the noxious half life of the monster. Knowledge brings no happiness. [bold = my emphasis]

One notes that the first line in the first 1818 edition is a reference to current scientific discovery:

> The event on which this fiction is founded has been supposed, by Dr. Darwin, and some of the physiological writers of Germany, as not of impossible occurrence.[*]

....

[*] Although unsigned, this preface is by Percy.

One cannot readily recall any previous novel in English striking this primal note. *Frankenstein* should, one fantasises, have been printed on litmus paper.

One should, however, be cautious in one's claims for *Frankenstein*. Science fiction ('the shape of things to come', as H.G. Wells called it) is no more likely to be good science than historical fiction good history. What Mary Godwin knew about science in 1816 she had mainly picked up from men like her father, her future husband, and Percy's new close friend Byron. And desultory reading. Chances are she knew as much, in depth, about the then-current quarrel between the materialists and the vitalists about the 'principle of life' as I (or you, perhaps) know in any depth about Schrödinger's Cat, Murray Gell-Mann's quark, or Tom Kibble's cosmic strings. But what matters is that she knew enough to write Aldiss's 'first real work of science fiction'.

The proof of the pudding is in the imitation. Few novels have been more seminal than *Frankenstein*. Every great SF writer, Aldiss fantasised (in *Frankenstein Unbound*), makes love to Mary Shelley. Yet it is not a perfectly written work – who would expect an eighteen- to nineteen-year-old to rival Austen at her peak? And, indeed, is *Frankenstein* entirely Mary's own work? Not everyone grants that.

It is clear on the manuscript page that Percy Shelley made thousands of stylistic changes to his wife's work. Perhaps Byron and Polidori said this and that and were taken notice of in Mary's own revisions. One will never know what was conveyed conversationally at Villa Diodati and in the nearby cottage the Shelleys and Claire were lodging in.* But the balance of evidence is that Mary Wollstonecraft Shelley is what the title of the latest biography, by Fiona Sampson, calls her: *The Girl Who Wrote Frankenstein* (2018).†

Post-1960s feminism has opened posterity's eyes as to how the story can be read. Mary, though not yet 21 when *Frankenstein* was published, had by then undergone two illegitimate births. One can sense postnatal revulsion in the chapter where Victor Frankenstein 'gives birth' in his 'workshop of filthy creation' (later the Monster calls himself 'an abortion'). The workshop of filthy creation can be pictured as the lovers' bed – and months later,‡ the marital bed, the birthing bed and, in some unlucky cases, the place where babies are born only to die. *Frankenstein* is a novel that has challenged every generation, each of which has read it differently. And thank God for rain, say I.

....

* One novelist has convincingly tried: Benjamin Markovits in *Imposture* (2007).

† A monograph whose title knowingly contradicts John Lauritsen's *The Man Who Wrote Frankenstein* (2007).

‡ Victor's Creature has five months' gestation, as did Mary's first child, Clara, who died two weeks after her premature birth on 6 March 1815.

Mary Shelley: A Brief Life

Mary Godwin was born in north London in 1797, daughter of William Godwin and Mary Wollstonecraft. He was the author of *An Enquiry Concerning Political Justice* (1793); she was the author of *A Vindication of the Rights of Woman* (1792). Mary never knew her mother, who died of puerperal fever a week after her daughter's birth. Natal trauma scenarios haunted Mary through life and are central to *Frankenstein*.

Mary grew up with a half-sister, Fanny, the illegitimate daughter of her mother. William Godwin then remarried and brought another illegitimate stepsister, Claire Clairmont, into the family. Whatever their rights, there was a plurality of women at 29 The Polygon, Somers Town.

It was an educational advantage for Mary that the family's penury meant most of her learning happened there. Books and radical ideas were as everyday items as breakfast – and more plentiful. Godwin never made money from his writings. As his only legitimate daughter, Mary was her father's favourite (but not that of her hated stepmother). William took unusual pains to cultivate Mary's mind.

Among a range of other subjects, he had her tutored in Latin and Greek. Orthodox educational opinion of the time would have likened it to teaching dogs trigonometry. In her

1831 preface to *Frankenstein*, Mary recalls 'writing stories' from her earliest years. Mary was a published author (with a short poem) at the age of twelve, and she was (her father recorded) as pretty as she was intellectually precocious.

Prominent thinkers and leaders of the Romantic movement made it a point to visit William Godwin. The most important date in Mary's young life was 11 November 1812, when she met Percy Bysshe Shelley and his wife Harriet, who were making a *de rigueur* visit. Shelley was a financial benefactor to the ever hard-up philosopher. Over the next two years he and Mary fell in love. She was barely sixteen, he was in his early twenties.

What did she look like in early life? Trelawny tells us that:

The most striking feature in her face was her calm grey eyes; she was rather under the English standard of woman's height, very fair and light-haired, witty, social, and animated in the society of friends, though mournful in solitude.

The couple duly eloped, without Godwin's permission, in July 1814 and left for Europe – currently in its pre-Waterloo lull. Shelley's pregnant wife and child were not wanted on the trip. (Shelley was no novice at this kind of escapade: Harriet Westbrook had only been sixteen when he had eloped with her to Scotland.) The product of this free-love honeymoon, the poem 'Mont Blanc' – and connection with Mary – marks a palpable growth in Shelley's poetry. But they ran out of money and returned, to public obloquy, in September, by which time Mary was pregnant.

The child (born in February 1815) died soon after birth. Shelley had, for love, lost not merely public respect but his private wealth. However, things looked up with a handsome bequest from his grandfather and the couple retired to a comfortable house in Windsor (lyricised in Mary's later novel, *The Last Man*). Their second child, William, was born in 1816 – still some months before his parents married. Their marriage was not a happy event – only being made possible by virtue of the heavily pregnant Harriet drowning herself in the Serpentine in Hyde Park. It was a month before her decomposed body was discovered, allowing Percy and Mary to legitimise their union. The Shelleys then took flight again.

There ensued the creative cauldron at Villa Diodati – the 'league of incest', as moralists of the time called it (because of Byron's earlier rumoured affair with his half-sister). Unlike her husband, who kept urging her towards rational adultery, Mary was a believer in neither free love nor Byronic recklessness. There were good reasons not to be. On the way to Switzerland they were accompanied by Mary's stepsister Claire Clairmont, pregnant and half-abandoned by Byron. Mary was still nursing her four-month-old son.

Alongside Lake Geneva, during this 'wet ungenial summer', the company of writers enlivened their confinement in the villa with ghost stories. Mary, momentously, contributed *Frankenstein* as part of the fun.

One says fun, but there was an overhanging sense of gloom – apocalyptic weather, public obloquy, shame. The creative mood in which *Frankenstein* was created had dark, sometimes eerie undercurrents. As Brian Aldiss puts it:

> Algolagnia* was certainly not absent from Mary's make-up. She wrote *Frankenstein* with her baby son William by her side; yet she makes the monster's first victim a little boy called William, Victor's younger brother. 'I grasped his throat to silence him and in a moment he lay dead at my feet. I gazed at my victim, and my heart swelled with exultation and hellish tri-umph.' ... Her little William ('Willmouse') died in the summer of 1819.

Over the next few years, the Shelleys were largely nomads in Italy. Ostensibly, the Mediterranean climate was kind to Percy's lungs. Italy was, however, less kind to little Clara Shelley's bowels, and the poor child died in infancy of dysentery.

Mary was again pregnant while watching her daughter die and sank into profound depression. Novels were, amidst all this domestic catastrophe (Percy, under the banner of free love, was never a faithful husband), taking form in her mind and in her notebooks; they would include the Italy-set *Valperga* (pub-lished in 1823) and the remarkable study of father–daughter

---

* Gaining sexual pleasure through inflicting pain on oneself masochistically or others sadistically.

incest *Mathilda*, written 1819–20 but not published until 1959. It has raised suspicion about the childhood relationship of Mary and her father William.

Mary's fourth child, Percy, would, mercifully, survive. His father did not. Percy Bysshe Shelley was drowned in a squall, sailing in the Gulf of Spezia. The young widow devoted the remainder of her life to the two Percys (her son William had also died, of malaria, in 1819). She installed herself as the custodian of her husband's literary legacy and – with financial help from Percy's family, long estranged but now partly reconciled – her son's education.

Percy junior was destined to be the inheritor of a title and a fortune. The family insisted, using the lever of a £250 p.a. allowance, on Mary and her son returning to England, where she was unhappy and chronically lonely and he was turned into exactly the kind of Englishman his father detested. Nor were Mary's relations with her father always good, although he did get the second edition of *Frankenstein* published for her.

Mary's financial situation eased when young Percy succeeded to the family title in 1844. She was not, however, to enjoy many happy years, dying of a brain tumour when still in her early fifties. Her radiant beauty had been wiped out by smallpox some while before. Everything, even death and decay, happened to Mary Shelley too young. She published novels in the 1820s and 1830s – most of them with the 'Prince of Puffers', Henry Colburn, for cash down and not much of it. Fiction was no longer a parlour game for her.

The most interesting of Mary Shelley's later novels is *The Last Man*. The action is set in the last years of the 21st century. England has become a republic. The abdicated royal family figure centrally around the person of the anchorite philosopher-narrator Lionel Verney. Shelley and Byron appear under thinnest disguise.

The third volume (the climax is tediously late in coming) features a worldwide plague which provokes first anarchy (the Irish make a spirited assault on Albion), then universal death to the human race. Lionel is left, a Robinson Crusoe of the future, the sole survivor of the 'merciless sickle'.

Conceptually *The Last Man* is, like *Frankenstein*, strikingly original. And, clearly enough, it allegorises Mary's late-life loneliness. But, as a story, it is sawdust – and unimaginative. Nautical transport two centuries hence is still by sail and wars are fought with the sword. Nor, it would seem, has medicine made great progress.

A stronger case can be mounted for *Mathilda*. The dying heroine narrates her father's incestuous advances on her and her love for the young poet, Woodville.

The blunt fact is that nothing Shelley wrote after *Frankenstein* is anywhere as good. Why? The male chauvinist reply is that her husband helped her out. Without Percy she was only half a writer. But so, most likely, would he have been without her. A more likely explanation of her falling off somewhat is that her later life was too much for her. Too much for anyone.

Where did Mary Godwin's 'hideous idea' come from?

⊘⊱⊘

W hat Henry James called a novel's 'germs' (ideas from inside the author), or *données* (inspiration from outside) are elusive things – harder to catch than soap bubbles. Shakespeare, if we credit *The Merchant of Venice*, would agree:

> Tell me where is fancy bred,
> Or in the heart or in the head?
> How begot, how nourished?

If we go along with what Mary says in her 1831 preface *Frankenstein* was 'begot' in a dream – beds being the best place for begetting. That dream had been 'nourished' by listening, in dutiful womanly 'silence', to 'long conversations' between Byron and Shelley about scientific-philosophical things. Her father had also been a brilliant, instructive, loudmouth.

Her own occasional attendance (there can have been few young women in the audiences) at scientific lectures, along with her private reading and her conversations with scientists stocked her mind with nuggets of hard information.

Mary recorded in her journal, in 1816 (the year she hatched the Ur-*Frankenstein*), that she was reading Humphry Davy's *Chemistry*, a transcript of his earlier London lectures which revolutionised the scientific thinking of the time. On the basis of this one mention (there's little other evidence of her reading science), critics have concluded that Mary Godwin was, if nothing else, curious about what was going on at the cutting edge. There is no direct mention of the contemporary disputes and scientific breakthroughs in *Frankenstein* – although it is plausibly suggested by critics that the conversations Mary (over)heard between Byron and Percy on the scientific topics of the day were formative. Victor, at Ingolstadt, comes to realise that 'Chemistry is that branch of natural philosophy in which the greatest improvements have been made'; Professor Waldman, a chemist, blows away Victor's alchemical fantasies.

The need to compose a pastime spine-chiller for the rainy Swiss summer of 1816 was Byron's diktat. The guidepost, as mentioned previously, was the French translation of a German *Gespensterbuch* (book of ghost stories), by Jean-Baptiste Benôit Eyriès, called *Fantasmagoriana*. Telling connections with *Frankenstein* have been detected.* But since there was only one copy of the volume available at Villa Diodati, it is likely that some of the reading was skimped, or second-hand.

And then came, as Mary recalled in her 1831 preface, the inspirational nightmare:

....

* For a lively discussion of the topic online see, http://www.romtext.org.uk/ frankenstein-and-fantasmagoriana-an-introductory-blog/

Night waned upon this talk, and even the witching hour had gone by, before we retired to rest. When I placed my head on my pillow, I did not sleep, nor could I be said to think. My imagination, unbidden, possessed and guided me, gifting the successive images that arose in my mind with a vividness far beyond the usual bounds of reverie. I saw—with shut eyes, but acute mental vision,—I saw the pale student of unhallowed arts kneeling beside the thing he had put together. I saw the hideous phantasm of a man stretched out, and then, on the working of some powerful engine, show signs of life, and stir with an uneasy, half vital motion. Frightful must it be; for supremely frightful would be the effect of any human endeavour to mock the stupendous mechanism of the Creator of the world. His success would terrify the artist; he would rush away from his odious handywork, horror-stricken. He would hope that, left to itself, the slight spark of life which he had communicated would fade; that this thing, which had received such imperfect animation, would subside into dead matter; and he might sleep in the belief that the silence of the grave would quench for ever the transient existence of the hideous corpse which he had looked upon as the cradle of life. He sleeps; but he is awakened; he opens his eyes; behold the horrid thing stands at his bedside, opening his curtains, and looking on him with yellow, watery, but speculative eyes.

I opened mine in terror. The idea so possessed my mind, that a thrill of fear ran through me, and I wished to exchange the ghastly image of my fancy for the realities around. I see them still; the very room, the dark *parquet*, the closed shutters, with the moonlight struggling through, and the sense I had that the glassy lake and white high Alps were beyond. I could not so easily get rid of my hideous phantom; still it haunted me. I must try to think of something else. I recurred to my ghost story, my tiresome unlucky ghost story! O! if I could only contrive one which would frighten my reader as I myself had been frightened that night!

Swift as light and as cheering was the idea that broke in upon me. 'I have found it! What terrified me will terrify others; and I need only describe the spectre which had haunted my midnight pillow.' On the morrow I announced that I had *thought of a story*. I began that day with the words, *It was on a dreary night of November*, making only a transcript of the grim terrors of my waking dream.

One catches a distinct whiff of gothic trope here. It reads like one of Mary's finer pieces of mid-career fiction. Too 'tremendous' to be true.

The founding novel of the gothic genre to which *Frankenstein* belongs, Horace Walpole's *The Castle of Otranto* (1764), is also presented to the reader as something initially dreamed, not composed:

I waked one morning in the beginning of last June
from a dream, of which all I could recover was, that
I thought myself in an ancient castle (a very natural
dream for a head filled like mine with Gothic story)
and that on the uppermost banister of a great staircase I saw a gigantic hand in armour. In the evening I
sat down and began to write, without knowing in the
least what I intended to say or relate.

Almost certainly Mary had somewhere lodged in her mind
another dream-given work of literature: Coleridge's 'Kubla
Khan' – more particularly the preface, printed with the poetic
fragment:

In the summer of the year 1797, the author [Coleridge
is writing of himself], then in ill health, had retired
to a lonely farmhouse between Porlock and Linton,
on the Exmoor confines of Somerset and Devonshire.
In consequence of a slight indisposition, an anodyne
had been prescribed, from the effects of which he fell
asleep in his chair at the moment that he was reading
the following sentence, or words of the same sub-
stance, in *Purchas's Pilgrimage*: 'Here the Khan Kubla
commanded a palace to be built, and a stately garden
thereunto. And thus ten miles of fertile ground were
inclosed with a wall.' The author continued for about
three hours in a profound sleep, at least of the external senses, during which time he has the most vivid

confidence that he could not have composed less than from two to three hundred lines; if that indeed can be called composition in which all the images rose up before him as things, with a parallel production of the correspondent expressions, without any sensation or consciousness of effort. On awaking he appeared to himself to have a distinct recollection of the whole, and taking his pen, ink, and paper, instantly and eagerly wrote down the lines that are here preserved. At this moment he was unfortunately called out by a person on business from Porlock, and detained by him above an hour, and on his return to his room, found, to his no small surprise and mortification, that though he still retained some vague and dim recollection of the general purport of the vision, yet, with the exception of some eight or ten scattered lines and images, all the rest had passed away like the images on the surface of a stream into which a stone has been cast, but, alas! without the after restoration of the latter!

No persons from Porlock visited to interrupt Mary's dream, thank goodness.

Coleridge is a doubly relevant reference here, as Anne K. Mellor instructs us:

On Sunday, August 24, 1806, when Coleridge and Charles and Mary Lamb came to tea and supper, [Mary Godwin, then aged nine] heard Coleridge himself recite 'The Rime of the Ancient Mariner', an event she never forgot.

Ever the over-hearer of men, Mary hid behind a sofa to listen, invisibly, to the poet recite.

Most assuredly that 'event' was still with her when 'dreaming up', reciting, and writing down *Frankenstein* several years on. There are any number of Coleridgean echoes, flagrantly anachronistic quotations, and settings in the novel drawn from the 'Rime'. The Walton polar voyage, within which the kernel narrative is framed, borrows imagery from the poem, as Coleridge himself borrowed his icy imagery of the polar south from Frederick Martens.* Walton himself is made to quote Coleridge's poem, five years before it was published.[†]

The image of Coleridge's 'alien' mariner, who has gone through 'life-in-death', feeds, one suspects, into the depiction of the Creature, born live from dead parts, and himself a doughty mariner. Six years old at his death, the Creature can hardly be called 'ancient'. But perhaps Creature years, like dog years, are multiples of human years.

There is a 'buried' source for *Frankenstein*. Literally. A gravestone, the leaden coffin beneath it and the body within the coffin. Mary and Percy met, as lovers, over the tomb of

....

* It is likely Mary had also read accounts of polar exploration in George Anson's 1748 *Voyage Round the World.*

[†] 'I shall kill no albatross' he says, after quoting the poem in Letter II. Walton's voyage takes place in the mid-1790s (see the chronological plot summary on page 51); the poem was published in 1798.

her mother – killed by Mary's childbirth – in the churchyard behind St Pancras Old Church in Camden, London. It is not one of the more famous literary resting places, such as Kensal Green or Highgate. But it is secluded, which is what lovers want. Twenty-one-year-old Percy and sixteen-year-old Mary had secret trysts over Wollstonecraft's remains, from early 1814.

The trysts, on consecrated ground, between these two avowed atheists, were clandestine. Outlaw almost. He was married to Harriet Westbrook Shelley, with whom he had fallen in love two years earlier. They eloped when Harriet, like Mary, was aged sixteen. Mary needed to be discreet because although her philosopher father liked his disciple Percy (and borrowed shamelessly from him), he would never approve of his daughter, barely past puberty, embarking on scandalous adulteries which would surely disgrace the name of Godwin. His free thinking did not extend that far.

Mary hated her stepmother (a 'filthy' woman, she thought, shuddering at the thought of her in bed with her beloved father) and revered the mother she never knew except by her writing and family legend. As a girl she piously read Wollstonecraft's works over her remains in St Pancras. There were, however, unhappy suspicions it was impossible to suppress. Was Mary (Wollstonecraft) actually there a few feet down?

Since the 1752 'Murder Act' the use of convicted murderers' bodies had been permitted for the purpose of advancing the science of anatomy. The Act was justified, theologically, as a 'peculiar mark of infamy' to be added to the punishment of hanging. It effectively made the dissection of all murderers compulsory.*

In the early 19th century, with the growth of teaching hospitals and the influence of the Royal College of Surgeons, the need for tuitional corpses outgrew what the rope could supply. Women's corpses were in particularly short supply, they being less murderous than men. In the service of anatomical learning, grave robbing was winked at by the authorities, and St Pancras graveyard, close as it was to the leading London hospitals, was for decades a prime site for corpse snatching – young pre-menopausal females being a particular prize.

Mary Wollstonecraft's grave, a low tableted rectangle, was a choice target. It had no 'mortsafe' (protective railings). There was no effective night security in the church grounds. The top slab could have been easily prised with a crowbar, then reclosed.

'Resurrectionists', the corpse retailers were called. In *A Tale of Two Cities*, set at the period Mary Wollstonecraft (aged 38, in 1797) died, Dickens alludes to St Pancras as a favoured site by body snatchers such as Jerry Cruncher, with their impious shovels.

Mary's fears about her mother's remains were revived at Villa Diodati, with John Polidori present. He had qualified in Edinburgh (Britain's most notorious centre for grave robbing) and had learned his sawbones craft as a trainee doctor on dead

....
* See Tim Marshall, *Murdering to Dissect: Grave-robbing*, Frankenstein *and the Anatomy Literature* (1996).

bodies of dubious provenance. He must surely have talked about it when the topic of *Schauerromanen* came up. Mary lived in terror that her mother's body had been 'resurrected' for the education of young Polidoris. Was her mother still there, in 1814, under the dull grey, lichened stone commemorating her? Or had her body been posthumously violated?

Mary's father had taught her to read by tracing the letters on that gravestone.* Morbid instruction. Love, death and literature would be the three strands coiling round young Mary's life and her first venture into fiction. It is romantically conjectured she and Percy first made love by her mother's grave in 1814. An unattractive fancy.

Wherever it happened, Mary was pregnant by June 1814.†
She and Percy planned their elopement, a couple of weeks later. His wife Harriet was also pregnant. It all blended into a concatenation of psychic transgression. There was adultery (actual or arranged) over the body of the mother the newborn Mary had killed. A place where she had learned to write, inscribing the words of death. And where, by flagrantly breaking the seventh commandment, while honouring the fifth, she made irrevocable her commitment to atheism. Alongside a church whose tuneful hymns, on Sundays, could be heard, bellowed by those more faithful than them.

....

* As described by Charlotte Gordon in *Romantic Outlaws: The Extraordinary Lives of Mary Wollstonecraft and Mary Shelley* (2015).

† Unlike Byron, whom he was yet to meet, Shelley seems not have used a contraceptive. 'Don't forget the cundums,' wrote Byron to his friend, John Cam Hobhouse, on his way to Switzerland in 1816.

Mary, daughter of parents who regarded themselves as paragons of modern ethics, was stealing an innocent (with child) woman's husband. Killing her, she may have later thought; as, by birth, she had killed her mother. And, at the very least, guaranteeing the name of Mary Godwin scandalous publicity, prurient gossip, and exile to come. All this before her life had really begun. One may readily assume this mix as having a formative influence on her first work of fiction. Children cast stones at Frankenstein's Creature. There would be many of the biblical kind cast at Mary Godwin, a woman taken in adultery.

The two graves of Wollstonecraft – she was, in point of fact, dug up in 1851 to be reburied in a family grave at St Peter's Church, Bournemouth – are still sites of pilgrimage for feminist admirers awaiting, ever more impatiently as the centuries pass, the 'Vindication' of women she demanded. Roll on. The St Pancras grave was also sentimentalised in the 19th century, notably by William Powell Frith's lush painting *The Lovers' Seat* (1877).

History is strange. Few of the buried can rest in peace in St Pancras soil. Thomas Hardy (a connoisseur of the life funereal) was employed, when a trainee builder and architect in London, in the excavation and exhumation of 2,000 graves to facilitate train entry to the enlarged St Pancras railway terminus in 1865. Progress. There survived the so-called 'Hardy Tree', with close packed tombstones round its bole, their owners gone who knows where. The excavation is echoed in the bitter later poem, 'In the Cemetery':

'You see those mothers squabbling there?'
Remarks the man of the cemetery.
'One says in tears, "'Tis mine lies here!"
Another, "Nay, mine, you Pharisee!"
Another, "How dare you move my flowers
And put your own on this grave of ours!"
But all their children were laid therein
At different times, like sprats in a tin.

'And then the main drain had to cross,
And we moved the lot some nights ago,
And packed them away in the general foss
With hundreds more. But their folks don't know,
And as well cry over a new-laid drain
As anything else, to ease your pain!'

Drains, trains. What's the difference?

Wollstonecraft's grave was not disturbed in 1865, nor in 2002 when thousands more corpses were dug up. Since her first resting place was adjacent to the church itself her memorial was not disturbed. Not even the convenience of rail travellers could justify demolishing the church supposed to have been the birthplace of English Christianity.

It goes on. Thousands of bodies (sprats in a tin) will be disinterred and a hundred trees will be felled (Hardy's, one hopes, spared) to make way for the HS2 railway link in the second and third decades of the 21st century. RIP always rings hollow in NW1 2BA.

An emollient HS2 spokesperson is on record as saying that they would 'ensure that we treat the site [i.e. corpses] with dignity, respect and care'. Let us hope so.

II.
THE STORY

What is the point of
Captain Robert Walton?

༺༖

The story opens with the explorer Captain Walton on his ship, within tantalising distance of the North Pole, witnessing a giant heading north at high speed in his sled over the ice, then, shortly after, an exhausted pursuer whom Walton will rescue and who, as he convalesces, will tell his extraordinary tale.

In her retrospective 1831 preface Mary Shelley recalled the dream which enabled her to join the narrative game in the parlour. And, posterity would think, go on to win:

> Swift as light and as cheering was the idea that broke in upon me. 'I have found it! What terrified me will terrify others; and I need only describe the spectre which had haunted my midnight pillow.' On the morrow I announced that I had *thought of a story*. I began that day with the words, *It was on a dreary night of November*, making only a transcript of the grim terrors of my waking dream.*

....

* As a brilliant medical student at Edinburgh, John Polidori was particularly interested in somnambulism and waking dreams.

The stories which the quintet exchanged among themselves (two, those of Byron and Shelley, soon discontinued, Claire's never begun) were necessarily brief – at most, 90 minutes reading aloud.* The Ur-*Frankenstein* which Mary recalls must have hooked the first listeners with its opening line: 'It was on a dreary night of November'.

A 'three-decker' (three-volume novel) such as that which the two Shelleys (he adviser and agent, she author and scribe) launched on the world on New Year's Day, 1818, was bulkier by magnitudes than what had thrilled the company at Villa Diodati. It was a commercial imperative for 'library editions' to be fat books. Two layers of padding were added in the published novel, delaying the line about the dreary night until a few chapters in. One layer is the prelude describing Victor Frankenstein's Genevese background, his mother's death, and his discoveries at Ingolstadt.

Wrapped around the whole of the three-volume narrative is an epistolary frame, in which Robert Walton recounts to his sister Margaret (will she ever receive the letters?) how his voyage into the Arctic deeps is progressing. Nothing much to report except icebergs, a homicidal giant, a dying scientist and a mutiny among his men who really can't see the point of going to the ends of the earth for the pittance Captain Walton is paying.

The Walton frame helps swell the wordage as library readers required and with its implied myth and symbolism enriched the narrative. Mary's understandable ignorance about life on

....
* The length, that is, of Polidori's 'The Vampyre', later published more or less in its original reading form.

the ocean wave leads to an occasional lapse. But research in books plugged most of the gaps. Immediately after Villa Diodati her journal for 16 November 1816 records 'read old voyages' – about the North West Passage and polar magnetism, 'the wondrous power which attracts the needle', one guesses.

The Walton frame raises a teasing puzzle: why does everyone go north in this novel? Why does it all end up the pole, so to speak, in blinding midnight sun? There is an unexplained geomagnetic pull straining the whole narrative and attracting all the main characters due north like a flock of instinctively migrating birds.

Why, one goes on to ask, does the Creature, of his own free will, go to the polar north to destroy himself by fire? It has been hinted that he – a giant – is of a kind with the pagan Norse 'frost giants'. If there is one thing in his short life Victor's giant loves and feels at home in, it is frost and ice.

Relevant here is Abigail Heiniger's explanation of the Nordic myth:

> Frost giants are not a part of the Norse pantheon in Valhalla. Rather, they live on the fringes of the world of men in a realm called Niflheim; it is a world of ice and mist separated from the human world by forests and mountains.*

The Creature's implied intention, once he reaches the pole, is

* Abigail Heiniger, as cited above (see page 4).

to find or create his Niflheim (mist home) and die in its sacred chill.

Why, though, does Victor, a delicate fellow not built for cold and hardship, follow his Creature through Siberia to the farthest North, after performing his final act of life-creation in the northernmost tip of Britain, the Orkneys? Victor has not a hope in hell (or the Norse 'Hel')* of killing the Creature, his avowed motive. The Creature has a sword, a gun and pistols, which he has used to purloin his sledge, provisions and dogs from terrified Inuits. Victor has come by his gear more decently but evidently forgot his dogs' provisions. All but one die (but oddly the single starved beast is still capable of pulling Victor's sled).

Vivified by ice, the Creature could swat his enfeebled would-be assassin like a fly. Victor would have a better chance with the polar bears. His rescue by Walton merely postpones his death for a few weeks and renders his ultimate end more comfortable. 'Ice' should be the cause of death written on the certificate signed by the ship's surgeon. Had Victor survived to make it to the pole he would have anticipated by 120 years the first human feet in 1909.[†] Their owners would have been mightily surprised to find a predecessor's faded Swiss flag fluttering there.

....

* Described in the 13th-century *Edda*, it is a freezing, not infernal region, under the rule of the synonymously named Goddess Hel.

† The 1909 team comprised Americans Robert Peary and Matthew Henson, and four Inuit men. Who was the first among them is disputed. See also Taylor Humin, https://prezi.com/logmjpdbprsv/polar-expeditions-and-mary-shelleys-frankenstein/ and Sarah Moss, 'Romanticism on Ice: Coleridge, Hogg and the Eighteenth-Century Missions to Greenland', https://www.erudit.org/en/journals/ron/2007-n45-ron1728/015816ar/

The creator/Creature rendezvous at the pole is mysterious. Another mystery is why has Robert Walton spent the six best years of his life working as a lowly seaman on whalers in order to train himself, and amass funds, to voyage to the pole? He perfunctorily suggests he is looking for the fabled North West Passage.

But Walton's deeper motive, we deduce, is to touch the navel of the world electrical, to find what turns the compass needle (and in this novel human beings) north. He will know why he has made the voyage when he is there. As he travels north, he feels he is fulfilling something deep in himself:

> I feel a cold northern breeze play upon my cheeks, which braces my nerves, and fills me with delight. ... Inspirited by this wind of promise, my day dreams become more fervent and vivid. I try in vain to be persuaded that the pole is the seat of frost and desolation; it ever presents itself to my imagination as the region of beauty and delight.

'Delight' is the word. His education, he tells us, was 'poetry'. Coleridge preeminently. One hears, too, an echo of Wordsworth's lines on Newton:

> The marble index of a mind for ever
> Voyaging through strange seas of Thought, alone.*

* *The Prelude* (1805). Mary evidently had a higher opinion of the 'Lakelanders' than did Byron.

Walton is as much an adventurer as an explorer.

There was a polar 'hysteria' in 1815 after the Napoleonic Wars – with all those ships and sailors suddenly lying idle. There were new worlds to conquer. Mary clearly caught the excitement. In 1819, as people were reading *Frankenstein*, there were five well-funded British polar expeditions. None reached the pole.

Mary's interest in things polar, as has been said, can be traced back to when, as a nine-year-old, hiding behind the sofa, she heard Coleridge reciting his 'Rime' and was caught up, for life, in what Francis Spufford calls 'the hazy love affair between the ice and the English'.*

Another force pulling everyone magnetically north is to be found in ancient 'Arktos' myths, of which the above Niflheim is but one. These myths fantasised what man – were man hubristic enough to try, and lucky enough to succeed – would actually find at the pole.

One principal myth, still believed as late as Elisha Kent Kane's expedition in the mid-1850s, was that there was a warm ocean up there with geothermal 'gates', if only they could be located and penetrated. An Eden, no less.

And what was it that frustrated every expedition made to the pole and kept doing so until the first decade of the 20th century? Was it, perhaps, some energy force – a reverse magnetism? Or was there, as the more devout feared, a divine prohibition against man's presumption?

....

* In *I May Be Some Time: Ice and the English Imagination* (1996).

As recounted in the ancient pagan Norse poem *The Edda*, the great Tree of Life, Yggdrasil, is rooted at the North Pole. It is 'the largest plant in the world', and man approaches Yggdrasil at his peril. So Captain Robert Walton discovers.

Where did Mary and Percy Shelley learn about Norse mythology? Bishop Percy's *Northern Antiquities* (1770) is the answer. That popular book was on their reading list in 1815, a few months before Villa Diodati. It was a translation of Paul Henri Mallet's *Introduction à l'histoire de Dannemarc* (1755). Bishop Percy it was who made Norse runic mythology a vibrant element in English Romantic ideology.

After he has seen the demise of the Creature and Victor, Walton accepts the cosmic prohibition against 'presumption' such as his and turns back. He is, he accepts, a mere mortal:

> The die is cast; I have consented to return, if we are not destroyed. Thus are my hopes blasted by cowardice and indecision; I come back ignorant and disappointed ... It is past; I am returning to England. I have lost my hopes of utility and glory; – I have lost my friend.

Once returned he will live, a sadder and a wiser man, to be united with his sister Margaret.

Was, then, the Walton plot merely narrative bubble-wrap to swell Mary's kernel story to three volumes? No. It is something worked into the plot which gives *Frankenstein* a deeper, more resonantly mythic tone. The romance of ice.

The University of Ingolwhere?

ௐ

A t the age of seventeen Victor is bundled off by his father to the German university of Ingolstadt. Here it is Victor encounters new scientific techniques which will allow him to realise the ancient dreams of the alchemists which have, for five years, entranced him.

Victor Frankenstein has his dreary November night of invention at the University of Ingolstadt. By the novel's calendar it is the late 1780s. He will be a young man to have changed the world. But so was the company of changers of the literary world at Villa Diodati.*

It is at Ingolstadt that, single-handed (not even an Igor or Fritz to assist him), Victor achieves the great synthesis between the alchemists of old (Paracelsus, Albertus Magnus, Cornelius Agrippa) and new, cutting-edge biology. As a philosopher-surgeon (his precise 'field' is never clear but chemistry dominates) he discovers how to reanimate dead human meat, skeletons and organs. 'Recycle' would be the more polite modern word.

Victor does not go on to graduate, outstanding student though he clearly is. Ingolstadt's devoutly Catholic custodians would certainly have expelled him (perhaps worse) had they

....
* Mary 18, Percy 24, Byron, 28, Polidori 21, Clairmont 22.

found out what outrageousness their pupil was up to in the name of science.

But around this period the university itself did things which outraged the Church and Bavarian state. The Ingolstadt institution was closed and moved out of town, by official order, in 1799. That date creates chronological queasiness in the narrative. Whatever else it is, the 'Prometheus' of the title is not 'Modern'. *Frankenstein* is analogous to a novel of 2018 being set, historically, in 1995.

The Ingolstadt University 1780s–90s periodisation pushes the current scientific issues which Mary was alert to into a vale of narrative implausibility. Science in 1816–17 had left that of 1780–90 looking decidedly dusty.

'All three serious reviews in 1818 mention that the novel is *topical*,' says Marilyn Butler in her densely informed article 'The First *Frankenstein* and Radical Science'.* Butler reckons as something central in the novel's thinking, although never explicitly stated in it, Mary's lively interest in the current quarrel, conducted by public lecture over 1814–19 at the Royal College of Surgeons, between the leading theoretic surgeons of the day John Abernethy and his former student William Lawrence.

The quarrel (it went well beyond 'debate') aroused public interest and centred on 'vitalist' and 'materialist' views on the nature and meaning of 'Life'. Did it, as the more orthodox Abernethy held, originate as something 'superadded', as God

....
* *TLS*, 9 April 1993.

'breathes' life from outside into the inert dust and purloined rib of Adam and Eve (along with the Edenic menagerie of animals around them)? Abernethy attempted to align electricity with the immaterial Holy Spirit. Animation and animus (literally 'soul') were connected.

Or was life, as the materialist Lawrence maintained, something corporeal? Inborn.

One can think of illustrative examples from contemporary fiction and film: Stephen King's *Pet Sematary*, for example, is vitalist. There is, the novel imagines, surviving potential for life, even in the dead and buried – if the right ceremonies and abracadabras are followed. But the reanimations which result are horrible. Kazuo Ishiguro's *Never Let Me Go*, by contrast, is materialist. You can patch the human body, as the novel fantasises, with any number of spare parts, conveniently stored in a sub-humanoid clone.

In *Frankenstein* the dispute sparks questions such as: 'the Creature clearly has a mind – but does he have a soul?'. If not, does anyone? Does he have a mind of his own, or is his extraordinary intelligence merely the legacy of the previous owner of 'his' ('their') brain? The early-century dispute over vitalism and materialism has been seen as a foretremor of (Charles) Darwinism 50 years later.

William Lawrence was a friend of and physician to Percy and Mary and she follows him in tending towards a materialist explanation of how Victor animates his Creature at Ingolstadt. But what about his second Creature? Supposition is artfully frustrated by Victor being so coy about how his operations, on which the story hinges, are carried out. Victor's justification is the horrors which would ensue should his techniques become public knowledge.* Victor is not, like his mythic precursor, a giving Prometheus.

As a novelist Mary is tolerant of anachronism. There are many other lapses in strict chronology. Readers, sensibly, let such things pass. So too does one let pass that this narrative of the late 1780s and early 1790s, conceived among rebels and revolutionaries in exile, makes not even the most passing reference to the French Revolution – even when Victor and Clerval are passing through the country, during the height of the 1790s *terreur*.†

But if radical science of the day is what *Frankenstein* ponders, as Marilyn Butler argues, why retroject the narrative to the dusty 1780s? Why not have a setting more congruent with cutting-edge laboratories and theory in the 1810s?

Answers suggest themselves. In 1791, when Victor is making his momentous discoveries, Luigi Galvani published *De viribus electricitatis in motu musculari commentarius*, 'proving' (as he claimed with public exhibitions) that bioelectronics was the life-force. He demonstrated the revivifying potency of electricity by making dead frogs' legs twitch under an applied shock. There is no reference to Galvani in the 1818 edition, but Mary inserted one into the 1831 reprint. It occurs when the

....

* The horrors are envisioned in Fritz Lang's *Metropolis* (1926). Lang had clearly thought deeply about how capitalism would exploit Victor Frankenstein's discovery to create a robotic, subhuman, working class.

† See the timeline given in the chronological plot summary on page 51.

fifteen-year-old Victor witnesses the great oak tree destroyed by lightning.

> Before this I was not unacquainted with the more obvious laws of electricity. On this occasion a man of great research in natural philosophy [not identified by name] was with us, and excited by this catastrophe, he entered on the explanation of a theory which he had formed on the subject of electricity and galvanism, which was at once new and astonishing to me.

Everyone at the Villa Diodati knew about galvanism. One speculates Mary may have toyed with a plot in which Victor Frankenstein beats Luigi Galvani to the punch.

Another nagging question. Why does Victor Frankenstein go 500 miles to study in Ingolstadt rather than the next-door University of Geneva? Or if it must be Germany, Göttingen, where Mary's admired Coleridge studied, and far ahead of Ingolstadt in scientific research.

Historically Germany's universities were, for centuries before and after, trailblazers in science and philosophy. Which is why young Hamlet ('the Dane!') goes to Wittenberg (where a certain Dr Faustus goes boldly into the unknown, in the spirit of Frankenstein) rather than the University of Copenhagen.

There are other plausible intra-narrative reasons why Victor studies so far away from his home. It is his father's decision. One's guess is that exiling his son may be precautionary. Victor's marriage to Elizabeth Lavenza, his adoptive 'sister', has been arranged in accordance with Victor's mother's dying wish. Neither young person, the novel hints, is enthusiastic about the forced match.

Victor's father notices the lack of enthusiasm and queries his son: 'you perhaps regard her as your sister without any wish that she might become your wife.' At another point in the narrative Elizabeth sends Victor a strangely cool letter, releasing him from the match, should he want release.

It is, Frankenstein senior may think, wise that the engaged couple be kept apart until they are brought to the altar, as his sainted wife insisted they should be. Therefore he sends Victor to far-off Bavaria until he reaches majority. For two years Frankenstein junior does not send a letter home – even to Elizabeth.

Another plot-logic reason for Ingolstadt rather than Geneva is that had Victor pursued his criminal experiments and graveyard raids in his home town, living at his parental home, it would have been impossible to maintain the secrecy his venture requires. 'What's that awful smell coming from your rooms?', one can imagine his father inquiring. 'And where, my dear boy, do you go every night with that shovel and sack?' And later, 'Who is that interesting eight-foot friend of yours, sleeping in your bedroom?'

There is a final reason for Mary Shelley choosing 1790 and Ingolstadt, bad fit as it is in other ways. Why did the authorities effectively shut down the Bavarian university in 1790? Because it was the headquarters of the 'Order of the Illuminati' – the enlightened ones.

The paranoiac secret society, modelled on the Freemasons and dedicated, as its name implies, to 18th-century Enlightenment rationalism, was formed on 1 May 1776 by Adam Weishaupt, a professor of law at Ingolstadt. It opposed theocratic, political and intellectual tyranny (on such things as scientific experimentation) advocating free thinking in every department of life. Weishaupt recruited hand-picked students as the nucleus of his organisation. Illuminati, like Masons, or Scientologists, were graded: novices, minervals, and illuminated minervals.

The Illuminati movement spread underground from Ingolstadt across Europe and its members swelled to thousands of the intelligentsia. Fancifully, it has been alleged to have been a *provocateur*, along with the *philosophes*, in revolutionary France.

The Society was banned in 1784 and Bavaria became too hot for Weishaupt. The University of Ingolstadt itself was closed in 1799 and moved to Landshut, where it could quietly decline into nullity and bother the world no more. The Illuminati live on, however, in popular legend and, it's thought by the gullible, in secret cells. They have been accused in modern times of clandestine, world-changing deeds – the assassination of JFK, for example. Queen Elizabeth II is said to reign as the symbolic head of the Order. Doubtless their secret icon is the corgi, as the Masons' is the thumbless handshake.

One can hypothesise reasons for pre-dissolution Ingolstadt figuring centrally in *Frankenstein*. It was a place where dangerous things happened. It would be impossible for a clever student there not to know about the Illuminati – and they, given what Victor is doing, about him.

Mary Godwin wrote the first, skeletal, draft of *Frankenstein* in days. Necessarily. The company was waiting eagerly. Having Victor at Ingolstadt during the Illuminati crisis, or passing through France during the Revolution were, for Mary, potential plot resources to be kept in reserve in the event that she might choose to make use of them in any enlarged *Frankenstein*. It's interesting to speculate how she might have done so.

One can spin a fanciful, unwritten plot. Victor is enrolled (as an illuminated minerval, of course) and encouraged by his Illuminati patrons. His experiment is attractively anti-religious. Or, alternatively, Victor, passing through Revolutionary France with Clerval, a couple of years later, does some creative joinery on the bodies and heads separated by Madame Guillotine. Marie Antoinette could live again.

TV serials like *The Wire*, one is told, which move as the spirit takes the scriptwriting team from instalment to instalment, have what are called 'pipes' dropped in the narrative in the event that a later turn of event may find them useful. If they're not used, no matter. Mary Shelley, one assumes, was, in her own way, a skilled pipe-layer.

Frankenstein:
A chronological plot summary

There are few dates given in *Frankenstein* and few period markers. Overall one can assume a time frame of circa 1769 to circa 1797, Mary's date of birth.

I have assumed that Victor is born in 1769 in Naples and moves with his family, less an aunt, to Geneva in 1775 (these facts are given in the 1831, not the 1818, edition of *Frankenstein*).

Victor's father Alphonse holds a mayoral position in Geneva. In 1782, aged thirteen, Victor comes across a work of Cornelius Agrippa and dreams of banishing disease from the human race. In 1784, aged fifteen, he witnesses the awesome power of lightning. What is it? 'Electricity,' his father says.

In October 1786, his father sends Victor to Ingolstadt University in Bavaria, possibly to clear his mind of all the alchemical nonsense. His mother intends that he shall marry his Italian cousin, who lives with the Frankensteins, Elizabeth Lavenza. In addition to Elizabeth his mother has adopted a young unfortunate, Justine Moritz.

Caroline Frankenstein, Victor's mother, dies from scarlet fever, contracted while nursing Elizabeth (who survives), on the same day (in October 1786) that Victor was due to leave for Ingolstadt.

From October 1786 to May 1792 Victor studies at Ingolstadt. In summer 1788 he makes his first discoveries and begins secretly working on his reanimation process.

In November 1791 the reanimation operation is successful. Victor has created life. The Creature runs off and finds refuge in the woods. The following day, Henry Clerval arrives, ostensibly to enrol as a student but probably to bring Victor, who has not written to his family, back to Geneva for his wedding.

Victor has a nervous collapse on Clerval's arrival and will not recover until March 1792. The two young men remain in Ingolstadt until May 1792 when Victor gets a letter telling him of the murder of his young brother William – assailant unknown. Seven months have elapsed since the Monster's birth. Victor has been six years absent from Geneva.

On his post-haste return to Geneva he finds that (thanks to the Creature's cunning) Justine has been set up for the murder of William. She is hanged in June 1792. Victor does not clear her as he could by telling the authorities about his Creature.

In August 1792 he fortuitously meets the Creature in the Alps. It was he who strangled William four months earlier and who incriminated Justine.

The Creature tells Victor his history since November 1791 when he blundered out of the laboratory into the woods.

He found shelter and, by observation of villagers, learned language. In late winter 1791/92, by spying and eavesdropping on a French family, he learned how to read and write. By spring 1792 he was an intelligent being. But the French family, when they saw what he was, drove him out. In April 1792, by examination of Victor's notes and journal, which he picked up leaving the laboratory, the Creature tracked his 'father' (as he thinks him) to Geneva in May 1792. Once arrived he strangled William and set Justine up to be hanged.

The Creature demands that Victor make him a female companion, promising that the pair will then depart for the wilds of South America, where they will live out their lives away from humans.

Fearful and remorseful – and perhaps wishing to postpone his marriage – Victor arranges, with the approval of his worried father, to take a two-year grand tour, 1793–95, in the company of Clerval – ostensibly to meet with English scientists.

The young men leave on their trip in August 1793. They travel through the Rhineland, Holland, France and finally arrive in England in December 1793. They spend three months in London and leave in late March 1794 for Perth, Scotland, and the scientific contacts Victor wants to meet. On the way north they spend April and May 1794 in the Lake District. (Victor loves the poetry of Coleridge and Wordsworth.) They arrive at Perth in June 1794. Victor leaves Clerval behind and goes to the Orkneys 'to finish my work in solitude'. Clerval knows nothing, apparently, about Victor's 'work' or the Creature.

In July 1794 Victor destroys the second creature he is making. The Creature abducts Clerval and murders him in Ireland. Thanks to the Creature's wiles, Victor is arrested for murder and imprisoned until October 1794 when his father arrives. He is acquitted and accompanies his father back to Geneva. It is arranged that his marriage with Elizabeth will take place in May 1795. The Creature murders her on the wedding night.

Victor dedicates himself to hunting down and destroying the Creature, who has fled north. By spring 1796 Victor is in Tartary and Russia tracking the Creature. Captain Robert Walton's ship leaves St Petersburg in June 1796. On 5 August 1796, hundreds of miles from land, he catches sight of the Creature and then rescues Victor, who is in a state of physical collapse.

The end comes on 17 September 1796 with Victor's death, the Creature's decision to kill himself and Walton's giving up his expedition.

Victor: mad scientist, deadbeat dad, or bad mother?

⚬⚬⚬

We are never precisely informed of what Victor does in his solitary Ingolstadt 'laboratory'. Films are explicit. Mary Shelley's artful swirls of narrative fog enable a variety of interpretations as to what Victor is, what he does, and why his creation, when he sees it, so appals him.

For 150 years Victor Frankenstein was routinely conceived by readers, critics and adaptors as an evil scientist. A man who, in Marilyn Butler's phrase, uses (male) science to make a baby without a woman, with the implicit aim of creating a world in which women are wholly dispensable – a gigantic male locker-room.

For the last 50 years he has more often been seen as a bad birth-giver – either as the mother who never gives her newborn the breast or as the delinquent dad who takes one look and walks out on his kid.

The different interpretations are testimony to the 'livingness' of Mary's novel, and its uncanny ability to collaborate with whatever the spirit of the age, the currently dominant ideology, or the cutting edge of science may be. The novel is a glove which has proved able to fit any socio-historical hand that reaches for it.

'Mad' science, as a literary idea, goes back to Christopher Marlowe's Faust, who abuses his ill-gotten knowledge for hedonistic pleasures – sleeping with Helen of Troy, most memorably.

My reading passion, between the ages of eight and ten (1946–48) was American superhero comics. Captain Marvel, Superman, et al. Stan Lee, the master creator of any number of comic superheroes (including Thor, Black Panther, the consorted X-Men and Spider-Man) was formatively influenced by *Frankenstein*. In a later life interview, discussing his invention of the Hulk, Lee recalled:

> When I was a kid, I loved the Frankenstein story. Not the book, I hadn't read that, but the 1931 movie. I felt the monster – the role that Karloff played – he was the good guy! He didn't want to hurt nobody. The poor guy was taken from the dead. He had a brain slapped into him and all these idiots with torches used to chase him up and down the hills ... and I thought, I bet it would be fun to get a character who's kind of a monster but he's really good. But just because he looks and acts like a monster people hate him, fear him, hunt him and try to destroy him.*

----

* https://www.youtube.com/watch?v=ETPYe6LEOIo

Drawing on Lee's observation, if the Frankenstein monster is the 'good guy', who then is the bad guy? His 'mad scientist' maker, of course.

What mad scientist can Mary have had in mind in creating Victor? Top of the list is Johann Conrad Dippel. This stupendous eccentric was in fact born in Castle Frankenstein* in 1673, and used its name, as an addition to his own, throughout his life.

Dippel studied theology, philosophy and alchemy – a heady mix – at the University of Giessen. As a scientist he is credited with genuine discoveries.† But Dippel did more Frankensteinian things. He created an alchemical 'elixir of life', known as 'Dippel's Oil'. A noxious brew resembling the tar water Mrs Joe likes to administer, as medicinal punishment, to Pip in *Great Expectations*, it did not, alas, prolong life. It was later proved effective as an insect repellent. Nonetheless, hope springing eternal in short-lived mankind, it sold well enough for Dippel to make an offer for Castle Frankenstein, then a hospital, in return for his secret formula. Rejected, alas.

There were rumours that Dippel dug up corpses and attempted experiments in metempsychosis and soul-transference – via a metal funnel between live and dead bodies, it's recorded. There is clearer evidence of his exploratory dissections of animals in search of what 'life' was. He has some

....

* A real place, located in Darmstadt in Germany. It is conjectured that Mary and Percy may have visited during their Rhine travels, prior to the novel's composition.

† Notably the dye 'Prussian Blue', still in use.

claim to be the last of the great alchemists. He died at Castle Wittgenstein. Another resonant name.

The coincidences are striking and critics quarrel over Dippel being a source for *Frankenstein* and Frankenstein.* The balance of scholarly opinion is that he wasn't. But the congruities are remarkable.

Another mad scientist often claimed to be inspirational is Giovanni Aldini, the nephew of Luigi Galvani, the electrobiologist Mary Shelley refers to in her 1831 preface (but not in the 1818 text of the novel):

> Many and long were the conversations between Lord Byron and Shelley, to which I was a devout but nearly silent listener. During one of these, various philosophical doctrines were discussed, and among others the nature of the principle of life, and whether there was any probability of its ever being discovered and communicated. They talked of the experiments of Dr. Darwin, (I speak not of what the Doctor really did, or said that he did, but, as more to my purpose, of what was then spoken of as having been done by him,) who preserved a piece of vermicelli in a glass case, till by some extraordinary means it began to move with voluntary motion. Not thus, after all, would life be given. Perhaps a corpse would be reanimated; galvanism had given token of such things:

----

* See Radu Florescu, *In Search of Frankenstein* (1975); Miranda Seymour, *Mary Shelley* (2002).

perhaps the component parts of a creature might be manufactured, brought together, and endued with vital warmth ... I saw – with shut eyes, but acute mental vision – I saw the pale student of unhallowed arts kneeling beside the thing he had put together; I saw the hideous phantasm of a man stretched out; and then, on the working of some powerful engine, show signs of life, and stir with an uneasy, half-vital motion.*

As mentioned elsewhere, Galvani had shown how electricity could cause movement in the legs of dead frogs. Aldini went a step further with whole human corpses – to wondering audiences. The most famous such show was performed on a hanged murderer, George Forster, in January 1803. Forster's corpse was taken warm from the Newgate gallows to the Royal College of Surgeons:

> There, before an audience of doctors and curiosity-seekers, Giovanni Aldini ... prepared to return the corpse to life.
>
> At least, that is what some of the spectators thought they were witnessing. When Aldini applied conducting rods, connected to a large battery, to Forster's face, 'the jaw began to quiver, the adjoining muscles were horribly contorted, and the left

---

* On the odd vermicelli reference, see below, page 68.

eye actually opened'. The climax of the performance came as Aldini probed Forster's rectum, causing his clenched fist to punch the air, as if in fury, his legs to kick and his back to arch violently.*

It is hard to believe Mary Godwin had not heard of the much talked-about Forster display.

Experiments like Aldini's pondered the question of whether the shock of electricity could enliven. It could certainly do the opposite. No one has ever been sentenced to 'life' on the electric chair. Benjamin Franklin, whose kite and lightning experiments Mary Shelley refers to in the novel, took his life in his hands to make his point about cosmic electricity. The problem was, of course (as Mary would have realised), that making musculature jump by an external, applied jolt was no proof of internal vitality.

Aldini's experiment, which required only very basic apparatus (wires, clamps, and voltaic batteries) was re-circulated at parlour game level. Seven years after the Forster show, Thomas Jefferson Hogg recalled an event at Oxford where he and Shelley were students. Percy

> proceeded, with much eagerness and enthusiasm, to show me the various instruments, especially the electrical apparatus: turning round the handle very rapidly so that the fierce, crackling sparks flew forth;

....
* As described by Mark Pilkington, https://www.theguardian.com/education/2004/oct/07/research.highereducation1

and presently standing on the stool with glass feet, he begged me to work the machine until he was filled with the fluid [i.e. electrical current], so that his long wild locks bristled and stood on end. Afterwards he charged a powerful battery of several large jars; labouring with vast energy and discoursing with increasing vehemence of the marvellous powers of electricity, of thunder and lightning; describing an electrical kite that he had made at home, and projecting another and an enormous one, or rather a combination of many kites, that would draw down from the sky an immense volume of electricity, the whole ammunition of a mighty thunderstorm; and this being directed to some point would there produce the most stupendous results.

Mary must have known about this scientific enthusiasm of Percy's (nicknamed, one recalls again, 'Victor'). But what is relevant is that the 'mad scientist' role, which in the popular imagination Victor filled for a century or more, was male. Females with superior powers were wicked witches whose knowledge was broomstick and black cat lore, not laboratory science.

This optic changed with the growth to authority of literary-critical feminism in the 1960s and after. *Frankenstein* lost its manhood. What took over were feminised (the term is not derogatory) readings of the text and a new gender ownership.

The revision was in fact radical. One of the leading feminist critics, Anne K. Mellor, read the text as a Wollstonecraftian fable on who owns reproduction:

> By stealing the female's control over reproduction Frankenstein has eliminated the female's primary biological function and source of cultural power. Indeed, for the simple purpose of human survival, Frankenstein has eliminated the need to have babies at all. One of the deepest horrors of this novel is Frankenstein's implicit goal of creating a society for men only: his creature is male, he refuses to create a female; there is no reason that the race of immortal beings he helped to propagate should not be exclusively male.*

The word 'stealing' hits hard.

Mellor uses the term 'bad mother'. 'Bad' because by abandoning any maternal responsibility Victor monsterises a baby who could, with parenting, and the creation of an Eve similarly well treated, have become the hope of the human race Victor, in his teenage innocence in Geneva, dreamed of.

Frankenstein is, it was asserted after the sixties, as centrally founded on reproduction, and its carnal processes, as *The Handmaid's Tale*. Margaret Atwood's early poetry collection,

---

* Anne K. Mellor, *Romanticism and Feminism* (1988). Other critics who have persuasively argued feminist readings of the novel are Ellen Moers, Sandra M. Gilbert and Susan Gubar, and Mary Poovey.

Speeches for Doctor Frankenstein (1966), is relevant. It conceives the Creature as a woman, talking back angrily to a man's world. One recalls Mary's description of listening 'silently' as Shelley and Byron conversed about science. A man thing.

Viewed in this sixties-and-after way *Frankenstein* intermixes gender protest with disgust – against the male 'act'. The key to understanding what is implied in Mary Shelley's genesis passages in the novel is physical revulsion with a traumatised vagueness.

It is a reflex and a rhetoric associated traditionally in Anglo-Saxon puritan discourse with two activities: sexual intercourse (and its variant, self-abuse) and childbirth (and its variant, abortion). Both of these are conventionally 'filthy' (the word is used, in the context of procreation, five times in *Frankenstein*).

Thus in Chapter 22, describing Victor's abortion of the Creature's intended mate:

> During my first experiment, a kind of enthusiastic frenzy had blinded me to the horror of my employment; my mind was intently fixed on the consummation of my labour, and my eyes were shut to the horror of my proceedings. But now I went to it in cold blood, and my heart often sickened at the work of my hands.

'Consummation' (sexual climax); 'the work of my hands' (masturbation). The description is sexually loaded.

Mary, unlike Percy, did not have the advantage of a manly Oxford education to acquaint her with the latest discoveries in natural philosophy. But she knew all about making babies. And the author of *Frankenstein* had good warrant for mixed feelings about sex and childbirth. A strikingly original analysis of the novel along these lines was outlined by Ellen Moers in 1974.

Moers read the 'creation' episode in Ingolstadt not as some alchemical transmutation (as in turning lead to gold), nor as a clinical scientific experiment. It was an expression of the 'trauma of the afterbirth'. Moers traced the experiences which, over Mary's short lifetime, conduced to a jaundiced view of motherhood. Mary Wollstonecraft Godwin was born on 30 August 1797, five months after her parents' marriage (as the Creature is born after a mysterious five months' gestation).

Mary's mother, Mary Wollstonecraft, died ten days later, of puerperal fever – uterine infection. Mary, in a sense, killed the woman who gave her life – or, as the young child may have thought in her gloomiest moments, her mother could not bear to live, having looked on her child.

Barely past puberty, Mary eloped to France with Percy Shelley in July 1814. Sexual intercourse began early for her. And her devirgination was unhallowed. In February 1815 Mary (aged seventeen) gave premature birth to a daughter who died a few days later. In January 1816 she gave birth to a son, William. (His death in June 1819 had an eerie significance. As Percy wrote: 'By the skill of the physician he was once reanimated after the process of death had actually commenced, and he lived four days after that time'. Death could be reversed.)

Mary and Percy did not marry until December 1816 (a few days after the suicide of Percy's first wife, Harriet, pregnant by another man). While she was completing *Frankenstein* in May 1817, Mary was pregnant with her third child, Clara, who was born in September. She was just twenty.*

Despite her free-thinking, rationalist, atheistic background, Mary may well have been ashamed of her irregular and busy sexual career. Her first unhappy experience of motherhood – which must surely have occurred before she was emotionally ready for it – was horrific. Mary's distaste for the business of procreation spills over, Moers plausibly argues, into the plot of her novel.

One can enlarge on this insight, and see the trauma extending beyond the 'afterbirth' into disgust at the whole 'filthy' mechanics of sex. Reading between the lines, the strong implication is that Victor creates his monster not by surgical manufacture, but by a process analogous to fertilisation and *in vitro* culture. And masturbation.

The resulting seed is mixed with a tissue, or soup composed of various tissues. The mixture is brewed until, like the child cut from the umbilical cord, it is released into life. Victor Frankenstein, that is, is less the mad scientist than the reluctant parent, or semen donor. He does not make his monster, as one might manufacture a robot – he gives birth to him, as

....

* Judith Chernaik deals with this tangle of sex and birth in her novel *Love's Children* (1992).

one might an unwanted child, the sight of whom fills one with postnatal disgust. His revulsion for his 'creation' may well, as Moers suggests, reflect aspects of Mary's own postnatal depressions and her distaste for the nasty business by which babies are made. Inter urinas et faeces nascimur, asserted St Augustine, bleakly. By dispensing with women as vehicles for babies, Victor has created a much more sanitary process – or so he fondly expects. No orifice required. No filth.

The principal warrant for this speculation is, of course, the flavour of the rhetoric. Had Victor Frankenstein been the geek scientist of later film fame, his creation would have been 'blasphemous', 'vile', 'outrageous', or 'an offence against law'. It would not have been, as Shelley repeatedly labels it, 'filthy'. It was a favourite adjective with her. Mellor suggests that Mary called her stepmother 'filthy' because she was sleeping with her father, thwarting Mary's suppressed incestuous longings. She was, one presumes, as disgusted with herself as with Mary Jane Clairmont Godwin, the hated woman who replaced beloved Mary Wollstonecraft Godwin.

Over the last century and a half one can see an interesting evolution in interpretation of the 'making the Creature' process. Early stage versions, from Richard Brinsley Peake's 1823 *Presumption* onwards, hampered by the limitations of theatre machinery, fell back on the standby of the 'elixir of life' device (flasks are easier to come by as props than the paraphernalia of laboratories). The electrico-robotic *Frankenstein* came in with the growth of the movie industry in the 1930s, and the Hollywood studios' no-expense-spared attitude to special effects.

In the 1970s, as a consequence of feminist rereadings of classic literary texts, a 'gynocritical' explanation was developed by academics, and *Frankenstein* became a central work in the formation of a canon of feminist literature.

So is Victor a mad scientist or a bad mother? Both. It depends on the date on your calendar.

Spaghetti?

꤮

W hat little the novel tells us about the animation of dead parts into a whole creature by Victor in his laboratory contains an odd lapse into pasta.

At the request of the publishers of the 1831 reprint of *Frankenstein*, Mary Shelley (as she now was, though widowed) was asked to write an introduction, which she did. Grudgingly, its first paragraph suggests.

One is grateful to Colburn and Bentley, the publishers. In the afterthought introduction Mary Shelley gave the authoritative version of the gamesome situation in which her novel, and Polidori's *The Vampyre*, came to birth.

Her account includes the following passage (already quoted, at greater length, on pages 58–9):

> Many and long were the conversations between Lord Byron and Shelley, to which I was a devout but nearly silent listener. ... They talked of the experiments of Dr. Darwin, ... who preserved a piece of vermicelli in a glass case, till by some extraordinary means it began to move with voluntary motion.

'Devout but nearly silent' flashes up a striking image of the 'young girl' (as she calls herself) overawed in the company of these eminent men. Polidori, a mere doctor, was similarly subdued.

In fact, Mary, as her journal entries at the villa testify, does herself an injustice. She was a participant in these high-end discussions, not an eavesdropper:

> June 15 ... Shelley and I had a conversation about principles, – whether man was to be thought merely an instrument ...

The Dr Darwin Mary refers to in her introduction is Erasmus Darwin, physician, poet and grandfather of the more famous Charles who took Victorian England by the scruff and shook all the religion out of it. But what is locally puzzling in the above passage is the word 'vermicelli' – which, as Wikipedia tells us, is thin spaghetti outside Italy and thick spaghetti inside the country. Whatever its girth, it's pasta and is not cooked in a test tube.

Mary Shelley's allusion is to the owlishly scientific notes Darwin appended to his book-length poem, *The Temple of Nature* (1803), an extravagantly periphrastic verse meditation on the nature of life: its origins, propagation and self-renewals.

Relevant to what Shelley writes is Darwin's note to a couplet in Canto 1:

> Hence without parent by spontaneous birth
> Rise the first specks of animated earth.

The prose 'additional note' is in an appendix entitled 'Spontaneous Vitality of Microscopic Animals'. The lines had clearly provoked protest, flatly contradicting, as they provocatively did, the account in Genesis. God had nothing to do with creating life: it was 'spontaneous' – itself only. Darwin mounted, in his note, an artillery barrage of scientific evidence and scholarly buzzwords:

Some of the microscopic animals are said to remain dead for many days or weeks, when the fluid in which they existed is dried up, and quickly to recover life and motion by the fresh addition of water and warmth. Thus the chaos redivivum of Linnæus dwells in vinegar and in bookbinders' paste: it revives by water after having been dried for years, and is both oviparous and viviparous. Thus the *vorticella* or wheel animal, which is found in rain water that has stood some days in leaden gutters, or in hollows of lead on the tops of houses, or in the slime or sediment left by such water, though it discovers no sign of life except when in the water, yet it is capable of continuing alive for many months though kept in a dry state. In this state it is of a globulous shape, exceeds not the bigness of a grain of sand, and no signs of life appear; but being put into water, in the space of half an hour a languid motion begins, the globule turns itself about, lengthens itself by slow degrees, assumes the form of a lively maggot, and most commonly in a few minutes afterwards

puts out its wheels, swimming vigorously through the
water as if in search of food; or else, fixing itself by the
tail, works the wheels in such a manner as to bring its
food to its mouth. [my emphasis]

What are vorticella? One turns (to save time is the excuse) to
Wikipedia, and its dauntingly informed definition:

Vorticella is a genus of bell-shaped ciliates that have
stalks to attach themselves to substrates. The stalks
have contractile myonemes, allowing them to pull the
cell body against substrates. The formation of the stalk
happens after the free-swimming stage.

There are five words in those two sentences I've had to look up
(the hard way, in the printed OED). Wikipedia goes on to tell
us that there are 200 kinds of vorticella – as many, one might
hazard, as varieties of Italian pasta.

There are two errors in Shelley's recollection. Darwin did
not carry out the experiments: he describes them, as done by
others. And in her use of the near-homonym 'vermicelli' (she
was, after all, in Italy, and it was one of the things she and her
vegan husband could ethically eat), 'Shelley simply goofed'.
Or so it's been suggested.*

The defence that, literally, vermicelli means little worms
doesn't wash. Vorticella are not worms, nor are they lively

....
* See Glenn Branch: https://ncse.com/blog/2017/05/vermicelli-vorticella
-0018542

maggots. I have not, incidentally, noticed Brito-Italian restaurants labeling their finer stranded pasta 'maggot bolognese'.

There is, however, another defence of Mary's vermicelli. Darwin (never one to spare words) writes a little later in the note:

> By the experiments of Buffon, Reaumur, Ellis, Ingenhouz, and others, microscopic animals are produced in three or four days, according to the warmth of the season, in the infusions of all vegetable or animal matter. One or more of these gentlemen put some boiling veal broth into a phial previously heated in the fire, and sealing it up hermetically or with melted wax, observed it to be replete with animalcules in three or four days.
>
> These microscopic animals are believed to possess a power of generating others like themselves by solitary reproduction without sex; and these gradually enlarging and improving for innumerable successive generations. Mr. Ellis gives drawings of six kinds of animalcula infusoria, which increase by dividing across the middle into two distinct animals. Thus in *paste composed of flour and water*, which has been suffered to become acescent, the animalcules called eels, vibrio anguillula, are seen in great abundance; their motions are rapid and strong; they are viviparous, and produce at intervals a numerous progeny ...
> [my emphasis]

Case proved – microscopic animals conceive as immaculately as the Virgin Mary. But *nota bene* (the Latinism is catching) 'composed of flour and water' – pasta, pasta.

It's not much of a defence. One hesitates to put Mary in the company of Sheridan's great word-mangler but she has perpetrated a malapropism.

Wanted: eight-foot skeleton

ॐ

Victor describes scavenging, in places of the dead round Ingolstadt, the body parts he will require to assemble his creature. But where, or how, does he come by a set of bones large enough for a giant?

Robert Walton's first sight of the Creature, in the frozen north, describes him as 'gigantic'. We are later given a precise measure of his newborn gigantism at his birth in Ingolstadt: eight feet.

In the illustration that forms the frontispiece to the 1831 reprint (the sole visual representation of the Creature Mary Shelley sanctioned – see page 101) there are various bones lying around Victor's 'workshop of filthy creation'. None looks appropriate for a man a foot taller than Kobe Bryant. (There are lots of slam-dunk basketball jokes in the 1991 film *Frankenstein: The College Years*.)

Where, then, did Victor get the skeleton his task needed? Assuming, that is, he 'assembled' not 'grew' (see page 65) the Creature, using parts no longer required by their dead owners.

There were eight-footers (some were circus exhibits) in the Regency period. They were rare birds, but they existed. Mary might even have seen with her own eyes some who qualified.

An exemplary case, for readers of *Frankenstein*, is that of Charles Byrne (1761–83, sometimes called O'Brien), the so-called 'Irish Giant'. His precise height during adulthood is conjectural, between 7 feet 10 inches, and 8' 4". His skeleton suggests 7' 7". Too tall by a full third, that is, for Tom Cruise (5' 7") to play him.*

Various folk tales were invented to explain Byrne's gigantism: one that he was conceived on top of a haystack – a sovereign heightener, Irish folklore had it. It is likely, however, he had acromegaly (an ailment of the pituitary gland) which leads to gigantism in those so afflicted. He was not a giant but a sick man.

Byrne came over to Britain in his late teens to make his fortune and, as a raree-show, did so. He appeared in stage burlesques. Just as, historically, 'Old Parr' was famous for his great age or Jeffrey Hudson ('Lord Minimus') for his dwarfism, Byrne became a byword for giants. Dickens alludes to Byrne in *David Copperfield* (1851), as does Thackeray in *The Irish Sketch Book* (1844). He died aged 22.

Byrne's subsequent career is relevant to *Frankenstein*. John Hunter, founder of the Hunterian Collection and Museum, was an avid collector of specimen dead bodies and skeletons. For research. Hunter believed that the Irish Giant would be a revealing target for dissection and attractive for display.[†]

....

* Cruise did, however, play Jack Reacher, 6' 5" according to Lee Child's books, in the 2012 film of that name.

[†] Hilary Mantel has written a novel, *The Giant, O'Brien* (1998) centred on the contest between Byrne and Hunter.

The Giant, in life, did not fancy the prospect of being disqualified for resurrection (in the Biblical sense) by corporeal particulation, nor being dug up by resurrectionists (in the Jerry Cruncher sense) to have his carcass picked over, like a Christmas turkey, by licentious London University students in the cause of anatomy. All offers of money from Hunter for the sale of his future dead body were sternly rejected by the Irish Giant.

Sick with consumption, and fearing the end, Byrne arranged for friends to dispose of him in a lead coffin at sea. He died in 1783. Not to be denied, the wily Hunter, having bribed one of Byrne's so-called friends, replaced the body with stones and smuggled the giant's body back, by night, to London.

Hunter stole it, in a word, as Victor Frankenstein criminally steals bodies and body parts.

Now that it was his, Hunter boiled the body, stripped off all tissue and fat (letting, presumably, anatomists see his prize) and two years later put the Irish Giant's articulated skeleton on display in his museum. It's still on view in a glass cabinet in the Hunterian Collection at the Royal College of Surgeons.*

Recently there have been demands that the Irish Giant's final wishes be respected. His DNA is still in his bones: the skeleton is still him, not a relic. The protests – the strongest emanating from Byrne's native Ireland – have been rejected. It would be like returning the Elgin Marbles of skeletons.

....

* I've drawn in the above on Andrew Connelly: https://www.aljazeera .com/indepth/features/2017/09/giant-charles-byrne-left-rest-peace -170918135540891.html

There is a last putative connection between the history of Byrne and the novel. Why does the Creature go to the North Pole to incinerate himself? Because he, like Byrne, who chose water, does not want his body to end up on the anatomist's table. It surely would.

POSTSCRIPT

Film-makers can also struggle with the eight-foot Creature, very often having to resort to lens and camera-shot trickery.

In James Whale's *Frankenstein* (1931), elevator boots and hidden mounting blocks made Boris Karloff lofty, if not quite gigantic (special effects would need a few more decades to pull that trick off). The actor's height off-screen was a modest 5′ 10″. The tallest actor to play the Creature was Glenn Strange, who appeared in three Frankenstein films of the 1940s. He was 6′ 5″ but not, alas, an actor in the class of Karloff, who reigns supreme as the celluloid Creature. Strange's most memorable moment on screen was being able to put the diminutive Lou Costello on his lap, in *Abbott and Costello Meet Frankenstein* (1948). Strange giggled so much innumerable takes were required to get the scene right.

The sewing machine:
a girl's best friend?

୬୧

Having gathered all the body parts he needs, Victor Frankenstein must find some way of joining them together. How? Superglue is not yet invented. Soldering would be manly but ugly. Mary, one can fancy, looked at her sewing box.

In the popular song 'The Sewing Machine' (immortalised by Betty Hutton, in the movie *The Perils of Pauline*, 1947), the titular machine is 'a girl's best friend' – one thinks of Mary Shelley's belittling reference to herself in her 1831 introduction, where she discusses: 'how I, then a young girl, came to think of, and to dilate upon, so very hideous an idea'.

The young girl Mary Godwin was home-tutored to a remarkable level in the knowledge usually reserved for men. But one purely feminine aptitude she must surely have had from an early age is skill with the needle and thread. If any of Percy Shelley's socks survive they will surely bear witness to that fact. Traditionally, British soldiers were issued with pouch darning kits called 'housewifes' or 'huswifs'. However, men who are not employed in the rag-trade, as it's called, are rarely handy with needle and thread.

In the 19th century the folk wisdom was that the only trades open to a young woman, however well educated, were governess, seamstress, or sex worker. But even girls of genteel and highly intellectual background, like Mary Godwin, sewed. Jane Austen's sewing box survives. Many of her manuscript materials don't. It was not merely housewifely, but often, as with Austen, a branch of domestic arts and crafts – all this, of course, 50 years before the 'girl's best friend', the domestic sewing machine, became available. What is it Charles Bingley says in *Pride and Prejudice?* 'They all paint tables, cover screens and net purses' – 'they' being the young, unmarried ladies in the drawing room.*

Even highbrow girls like Mary Godwin, we may assume, could mend their own blue stockings, their fingers as nimble as their grey cells. And, of course, darn the socks of the man and children of the house. The dexterity they acquired with the needle gave women, a pent-up labour force until the late 19th century, a huge advantage when sausage-fingered male office copyists (like Bob Cratchit in *The Christmas Carol*) went on the scrapheap with the invention of the typewriter in the 1870s. The typewriter girl (later 'shorthand typist') took over, going a hundred words a minute.

There has never, I think, been a survey of female sewing in literature. But one can point to a few high points. In the *Odyssey*, for example, Penelope uses her needle to make by day and unmake by night the shroud she is working on.

* See Jennifer Forest, *Jane Austen's Sewing Box* (2011) – a hugely informative book.

Her needlework keeps a host of predatory suitors at bay until Odysseus returns to settle their hash.* Lots of shrouds needed then.

Which brings us to Frankenstein's Creature. By what alchemical, chemical, or galvanic process Victor brings him into being is mysterious. But how he is put together is clear enough. He is sewn into wholeness from parts of bodies Victor has scavenged. The sewing line is quite visible on the dangling right hand of the only illustration Mary Shelley sanctioned (see page 101).

The question arises, assuming that the Creature is stitched up, what properly should he be called (in addition to all the other names he carries). Specifically, is he a quilt or a patchwork? Both are venerable needled artefacts and would have been known to (and quite probably created by) Mary Godwin.

As the Victoria and Albert Museum website informs us, quilt and patchwork are different things.

> Quilting is a method of stitching layers of material together. Although there are some variations, a quilt usually means a bed cover made of two layers of fabric with a layer of padding (wadding) in between, held together by lines of stitching. The stitches are usually based on a pattern or design ... Although quilting can just use basic running stitch or backstitch, each

---

* The point is made by Elizabeth Wayland Barber in *Women's Work: The First 20,000 Years; Women, Cloth, and Society in Early Times* (1995).

stitch has to be made individually to ensure it catches all the layers within the quilt. Where the stitching is laid down in decorative patterns, it can be extremely fine work. Popular stitching patterns have been given names such as 'Broken Plaid', 'Hanging Diamond', 'Twisted Rope' or 'True Lovers' Knot'.

More than the reader of *Frankenstein* needs to know, perhaps. But on the face of it the above would seem a fair description of what huswife Victor does in assembling his creature.

Patchwork is something different from quilting:

Although closely linked to quilting, patchwork is a different needlework technique, with its own distinct history. Patchwork or 'pierced work' involves sewing together pieces of fabric to form a flat design. In Britain, the most enduring method is known as 'piecing over paper'. In this method, the pattern is first drawn onto paper and then accurately cut. Small pieces of fabric are folded around each of the paper shapes and tacked into place (also known as basting, this uses long, temporary stitches that will eventually be removed). The shapes are then joined together from the back using small stitches called whipstitches.

If quilting is often associated with warmth and protection, patchwork is more closely associated with domestic economy – a way of using up scraps of fabrics or of extending the working life of clothing.

Unlike quilting, patchwork remained a predominantly domestic, rather than professional, undertaking.

There is appropriateness here as well. Patchwork is composed of fragments of material from here there and everywhere. Grave robbing, charnel house and slaughterhouse larceny in Victor's case.

Weighing up the criteria, Frankenstein's Creature is, I think, patchwork – although the element of upholstery (layering) might tend one towards quilting.

The important point is this. Before she was coerced, flatteringly, into writing and reciting *Frankenstein* Mary would, quite likely, have 'made' little that did not involve needle and thread. The vision of Victor sewing his Modern Prometheus would have slipped very easily into her mind.

It lives! It lives!
But what shall we call 'it'?

꒰ঌ

Christening the Creature Victor has just created is out of the question. But what name shall 'it' be called by? The novel never decides.

Genesis is one of the mythic 'footings' of *Frankenstein* – foundational texts on which the narrative rests.* When Jehovah (an entity whose awesome name is never to be mentioned in full by pious Jews) gives Adam animals for company in Eden (Eve comes later), the first thing Adam (newly created and newly named by his creator) does is to name them.

The animals are created, as in the children's song, 'two by two'. Adam, alone, is alone. Without a helpmeet (not a mate – the sexism is fundamental in the King James's Bible, hard to eliminate from later translations, and impossible to eliminate from Milton). It's an argument the Creature lodges against Victor, demanding he, like the lowly animals of the field, should be in a primal twosome. And multiply.

....
* Others are *Paradise Lost*, *The Sorrows of Young Werther*, Aeschylus' *Prometheus Bound*, and Godwin's *Political Justice*. Oddly, the Creature seems not to have known about the Bible and makes do with Milton.

Why do we name dangerous things? Because it creates an illusory sense of control. One sees the process in everyday life. America, for instance, names hurricanes that destroy her towns, as if they were babies at the font. It expresses the fond hope we shall have some power over them; befriend them, even. How can a 100mph wind called 'Betsy' harm us?

Monsters of the epic sort are routinely named. Homer, for example, gives us the one-eyed giant Cyclops 'Polyphemus'. The mudman of Jewish legend is called 'Golem'. The oldest narrative in English literature gives us Grendel and the even more fearsome Grendel's Mother. Caliban, born of the devil and the witch Sycorax, is Prospero's enslaved monster.

Why isn't Victor's 'thing', then, given a name? Not only is it unnamed, it is denied any species to belong to. But it has a gender: 'he', it is called. But how human is 'he'? Can 'he' mate with a human woman? The bits which compose him once did when in their proper place. But were some of those bits female? The brain, say?

Narrative, like nature, abhors a vacuum. In passing we note that Frankenstein's Creature is routinely mis-called 'Frankenstein', even by those who have read the novel. Anne K. Mellor makes the point that the error is 'intuitively right' – if, that is, we buy into doppelganger and Jekyll and Hyde theories. The monster morphs in and out of his scientific Maker in Stevenson's story. So too, it is argued, do creator and creature in Mary Shelley's story. Did, one wonders again, Victor mix some of his own seed (the 'work of his hands') into the animating brew?

The first name which the appalled 'father' Victor directs to his newborn is 'creature', closely followed by 'wretch', 'being', 'demoniacal corpse', 'miserable monster', and 'mummy'.* All this obloquy in three pages. But what is its 'proper name'? Or genus? A word count reveals that in the text as a whole there are: four 'demons', 64 'wretches', fourteen 'devils', 33 'monsters', 41 'fiends', 69 'creatures'. A chorus of unsystematic vilification. Take your pick.

The terms are appropriate in their different ways. 'Monster', for example, because the word comes, via Old French, from the Latin *monstrare*, meaning to demonstrate. The visible knitting, sewing, gluing and mismatched parts of Victor's monster demonstrate clearly enough that he is, to adapt the term, a man of parts. A thing of shreds and patches.

One can digress into biography to recall that names were touchy things for the author herself when she was writing *Frankenstein*. She was, for practical purposes, trinomial. As the consort (but not yet wife) of Percy she was 'Miss Godwin' or a brevet 'Mrs Percy Shelley' (what the starchier European hoteliers were presumably informed, when a double room was booked). She and Percy did not get married until 30 December 1816, in London's St Mildred's Church. The book was published an exact year and a day later.

---

* The latter is an interesting image. As Mary Godwin was growing up the British Museum was beginning to collect mummies (objects of perennial fascination to the public) on its way to creating the largest collection outside Egypt itself. Mary, a Londoner, must have gazed at them. See https://www.britishmuseum.org/PDF/Regarding-the-Dead-Chapter-9_02102015.pdf

Mary Godwin wrote the book, Mary Shelley published the book. Her mother's honoured name was one which she liked to insert into her own: 'Mary Wollstonecraft Shelley' – a mouthful, but one which is now generally approved. Her mother, in egalitarian spirit, called herself after marriage Mary Wollstonecraft Godwin.

Mary bore a short-lived child out of wedlock by Shelley – Clara – on 22 February 1815. She was promptly pregnant with the next, born in January 1816. The second child was called William and survived until June 1819.

The law was firm on the naming of illegitimate children such as Mary's first two. The child took the mother's surname – this to prevent later claims on any putative father's property. The law was not reformed until the 1960s. It is hard to think Mary did not refer to her first children as Shelleys.

Mary, now a married woman, was pregnant for the third time, aged twenty, when she completed the writing of *Frankenstein*. That child was legitimately Shelley. One could wonder whether this nominal haze swept over the novel's dramatis personae.

There is another little oddity. Film-makers, in general, do not like 'Victor'. In James Whale's classic movie, for example, Victor becomes 'Dr Henry Frankenstein'. One regrets the change because, as has been said, 'Victor' was one of Percy's nicknames.

In his trend-setting 1823 stage adaptation *Presumption; Or, the Fate of Frankenstein*, Richard Brinsley Peake imaginatively, called the monster '------'. Named him, that is, 'Who

Knows?' The gimmick pleased Mary, when she saw the play. One can see why. Namelessness facilitated identity fluidity. The Creature at different points in the novel self-identifies as Adam and Satan. 'I ought to be thy Adam, but I am rather the fallen angel.' Chalk and cheese theologically. Is he a monster, or a noble savage? Is he an evolutionary jump in the human species? Peake took the easy way out. The Creature is wholly mute in *Presumption*.

Stephen King, who acknowledges *Frankenstein* as the primal text of the genre he now dominates, pays tribute to Mary Shelley by calling his most chilling child-killing monster – what else? – 'It'. The son of 'Them', presumably.

The Creature, one may note, is gentler in his name calling. On first reading Victor's notes, in the woods, he calls him 'my father, my creator'. In that the Creature finally kills his 'father' one catches a faint Oedipal theme. Mary Shelley did not press it too hard. But it lingers in the mind.

Who makes the Creature's trousers?

◺

Having made his Creature ready for the outside world, a conscientious Maker would find some way of covering his nakedness. Victor Frankenstein is not conscientious.

The 1831 frontispiece illustration (referred to elsewhere and reproduced on page 101) shows the creature partly draped and physically impressive.* A raised right knee (in the novel he is lying flat) decorously keeps his private parts private. A towel, or small blanket, lies by his feet, draped across some surplus human remains. There is no clothing as such. A fully clothed Victor, dressed for the cold Ingolstadt November night (although he will stop for a snooze downstairs first) is halfway through the door.

The narrative, twice over (from Victor and later the Creature's recollection) is explicit about what happens next. Victor has a college apartment (God knows what the cleaners think about entrails, offal and newly exhumed skulls lying around – those students!). It is the study here which furnishes his 'workshop of filthy creation', occasionally called his 'laboratory' – meaning less a place of white-coat research than where he has been 'in labour', that is, 'giving birth'.

....

* For a detailed analysis of von Holst's design see below, page 100.

The appalled Victor, after seeing the awful thing he's done, retires downstairs to his bedroom for a troubled rest, leaving the roused monster to his (its?) own devices in the attic (where, one recalls, Rochester hides his monster of a wife and Dorian Gray leaves his monstrous self-portrait). A nightmare of erotically kissing his mother crawling with graveworms wakes Victor to find, by the light of the moon, the Creature has pulled open his four-poster bed curtains and is 'grinning' at him.

Victor rushes down to the courtyard, and paces outside the remainder of the night. At dawn, when the gates are unlocked by the servitors, he leaves the college to walk the rain-sodden streets.

A vivid verse from Coleridge's 'Rime of the Ancient Mariner' (several years before it would be published) runs through his head:

> Like one who, on a lonely road,
> Doth walk in fear and dread,
> And, having once turned round, walks on,
> And turns no more his head;
> Because he knows a frightful fiend
> Doth close behind him tread.

Victor is still on the move when, as fortune would have it (Mary Shelley was not an author afraid of coincidence) the Swiss Diligence arrives, and out steps – who else? – Henry Clerval. Joy. His friend remarks that Victor is rather pale, as well he might be, having just visited a monster on the world.

The bosom friends adjourn to Victor's college apartments. The Creature, it seems, has gone. Victor 'claps his hands for joy'. He rushes from the empty attic (empty, that is, apart from a few bones, entrails and unrefrigerated organs lying about) downstairs to Clerval, where, overwhelmed, he falls into a fit, and thence into a nervous collapse which will last months during which he raves deliriously about a 'monster'. No one pays attention. Just a nightmare.

Victor is nursed through his crisis tenderly by Clerval, who seems, in his bed care, to be something more than a mere friend. But wholly incurious about the contents of the study-lab. Henry came to Ingolstadt not merely to catch up with Victor but to study. That goes by the way.

What, though, has happened to the vanished Creature? As we later learn from his own mouth, he comes to conscious-ness as Victor leaves the room. At this moment the world is as William James describes: 'The baby, assailed by eyes, ears, nose, skin, and entrails at once, feels it all as one great blooming, buzzing confusion.'

He stumbles downstairs. Victor is at this point in the court-yard and out of sight. Day has dawned. He can walk. Other newborns might take two years to toddle. His superhumanity is beginning to manifest itself. At two years old the Creature will be scaling the bare face of Mont Blanc like a chamois and reading Goethe for relaxation.

Leaving Victor's apartment – it is now full daylight – the Creature leaves the precincts of the college and wanders the streets of Ingolstadt until he finds the safety of some woods on the outskirts. Here he refreshes himself with some 'berries' (in November?).

He has, he says, covered himself with some 'dress' of Victor's. But since he is 'gigantic', a full eight feet and as muscular as Michelangelo's Adam, it is hard to picture that he will find anything to fit. He 'exceeds the height of man'. Unmentionables will be a particular problem. He does not have the faintest idea how to put trousers on.

Fortuitously in the wood the Creature comes across a 'large cloak' under a tree, and is, we apprehend, decently covered at last. Nonetheless the collegians and citizens of Ingolstadt must be a strangely incurious folk. A giant, semi- or stark naked stumbles aimlessly through their town grunting and grinning, and no burgher takes any notice? Or perhaps they put it down to the usual student frolics: 'Nur ein nackter Riese. Man sieht solche Sachen jeden Tag der Woche. Verdammte Studenten.'

Victor remains in town, convalescent, for several months: no one, it seems, mentions this strange phenomenon in November. Or that the epidemic of morgue robbing has ended. What, one wonders, does Victor suppose has happened, when he recovers his mind?

Meanwhile, the Creature finds, in the pocket of whatever article of 'dress' he took from his maker's workshop-study, Victor's five months of working notes. The notes, with their journal entries, are what will enable him, when he learns to read (which he does phenomenally fast), to track his creator down 500 miles away in Geneva.

The Creature spends from November to the following summer in the woods where he learns, by inspection not tuition, about nature. A feat which would do credit to Linnaeus and von Humboldt. The villagers whom the Creature secretly observes instruct him on the nature of wealth, class, poverty, love and family. A degree-level course in social studies. All the while he is shoeless, with only the giant cloak to cover him, increasingly hairy and unwashed. No wonder children throw stones at him.

It was necessary for the creature to be clothed on stage in *Presumption*. He is given, in the pictured advertisement for the performance (see opposite), a toga. The cowering Victor is wearing an outfit apparently left over from a recent production of *Hamlet*. It's preposterous, of course. The monster should be naked, not dressed like a Roman warrior, sword in hand.

Mary Shelley could gloss over this little sartorial puzzle. Peake couldn't, and even less so film-makers, from the first 1910 Edison film onwards.* Whale's Karloff looks as if he has picked supersize items from the rack in the nearest charity shop. Branagh finesses it by making his Creature (played by Robert De Niro, height 5′ 7″) the same size as the star-director himself playing Victor (height 5′ 9″). Clothing no problem.

The mind roams back to two of the source texts for *Frankenstein*, the King James Bible and *Paradise Lost*.

....
* See below, pages 202–3.

Advertisement for Richard Brinsley Peake's Presumption.

The Almighty, having laid his terrible curse on the disobe-
dient apple eaters, copulators, and knowledge seekers, replaces
the fig-leaf skirts they have improvised, in their shame, with
something more appropriate for the land east of Eden (Nod,
as it's called). As Genesis puts it:

Unto Adam also and to his wife did the LORD God
make coats of skins, and clothed them.

A bit of a comedown for the supreme entity who has recently created heaven and earth – getting to work with his needle and thread. The Almighty, presumably, intends clothes to be the permanent mark of shame.

The 'coats of skins' (one recalls the Creature's 'cloak') also introduce killing into the world. God must have killed animals for their skins (Percy Shelley, we may recall, was an atheist and a vegan). The clothes Adam and Eve wear mean the first blood-shed in Eden, where previously the lion lay down with the lamb: both, in the fallen world, will be valued for their coats. There will be a lot more blood-spillage in the fallen world.

What, precisely, do we know of 'the process'?

༺ఈ༻

Victor is very tight-lipped about how he 'makes' the Creature. Would that we might see, as an appendix to the novel, the working notes the Creature purloins.

One of the tricks of the 19th-century novel trade was artfully withholding information. In *Wuthering Heights*, for example, readers would dearly like to know what has transformed Heathcliff from stable groom to moneyed gentleman in his two years' absence from Yorkshire. We shall never know. So too in *Frankenstein*. Mary (or is it Victor?) artfully declines to give detail about how the operation in the filthy workshop is done. It's a cunningly created black hole which sucks the speculative reader in but never lifts the darkness.

Deducibly Victor collects and arranges various materials for the act: but what precisely these materials are is not divulged. It's wrapped up in magnificent Gothic haze:

> One secret which I alone possessed was the hope to which I had dedicated myself; and the moon gazed on my midnight labours, while, with unrelaxed and

breathless eagerness, I pursued nature to her hiding places. Who shall conceive the horrors of my secret toil, as I dabbled among the unhallowed damps of the grave, or tortured the living animal to animate the lifeless clay? My limbs now tremble, and my eyes swim with the remembrance; but then a resistless, and almost frantic impulse, urged me forward; I seemed to have lost all soul or sensation but for this one pursuit. It was indeed but a passing trance, that only made me feel with renewed acuteness so soon as, the unnatural stimulus ceasing to operate, I had returned to my old habits. I collected bones from charnel houses; and disturbed, with profane fingers, the tremendous secrets of the human frame. In a solitary chamber, or rather cell, at the top of the house, and separated from all the other apartments by a gallery and staircase, I kept my workshop of filthy creation; my eyeballs were starting from their sockets in attending to the details of my employment. The dissecting room and the slaughter-house furnished many of my materials; and often did my human nature turn with loathing from my occupation, whilst, still urged on by an eagerness which perpetually increased, I brought my work near to a conclusion.

NB 'slaughterhouses' – i.e. animal abattoirs.

A number of interesting features stand out from the rhetorical swirl. Clearly Victor Frankenstein has undertaken fieldwork which would get him disbarred from the Royal College of Surgeons.

The most urgent feature of Victor's description is the emetic disgust and the narrator's irresistible urge to avert his eyes from his 'workshop of filthy creation'. It is a workshop lacking refrigeration or cryogenic apparatus. He begins his flesh-collecting in August. His workshop will smell ranker than Ingolstadt's seediest rag and bone shop by November.

'Reverse dissection' is Richard Holmes's happy phrase for what Victor is doing. One can't imagine the very young Mary attending one of the dissecting theatres in London's teaching hospitals. But it is easy to imagine her visiting John Heaviside's museum in Hanover Square in London. A privately rich surgeon, Heaviside was able to purchase interesting anatomical specimens. He regularly opened his collection to medics and 'respectable strangers'.

For a century yet there would be no refrigeration such as enables today's medical students to learn their trade on actual corpses (nowadays not supplied by grave robbery but voluntary in-life donation). Specimens in the early 19th century were preserved for display and teaching by drying (a complex business). Softer tissues were preserved in jars of wine and turpentine.*

Finally, on the fateful, dreary night in November the monster comes to life – not under the stimulus of some immense bolt of meteorological energy, but simply by opening his eyes

....
* See https://www.ncbi.nlm.nih.gov/pmc/articles/PMC3162231/

and shuddering, like any other newborn human. A veritable convulsion of nauseated disgust follows Victor's first sight of his animated 'baby':

How can I describe my emotions at this catastrophe, or how delineate the wretch whom with such infinite pains and care I had endeavoured to form? His limbs were in proportion, and I had selected his features as beautiful. Beautiful! Great God! His yellow skin scarcely covered the work of muscles and arteries beneath; his hair was of a lustrous black, and flowing; his teeth of a pearly whiteness; but these luxuriances only formed a more horrid contrast with his watery eyes, that seemed almost of the same colour as the dun-white sockets in which they were set, his shrivelled complexion, and straight black lips.

The mysterious animating operation is repeated later in the narrative, when Victor, against his better judgement, is induced to create a mate for his monster. He does so (surreally enough) in the Orkney wilderness. There are, apparently, no graveyards, anatomy theatres, or slaughterhouses for him to prey on in this northern wasteland. His island has only three huts, into one of which Victor moves himself and his laboratory equipment. Again we are told it is 'a filthy process' – and virtually nothing more, other than that the operation is even more loathsome than before:

During my first experiment, a kind of enthusiastic frenzy had blinded me to the horror of my employment; my mind was intently fixed on the sequel of my labour, and my eyes were shut to the horror of my proceedings. But now I went to it in cold blood, and my heart often sickened at the work of my hands.

But what, precisely, is that 'work'? Any reader's guess is as good as any other reader's.

What does the Creature look like?

ᜎᜎ

Film audiences know. Novel readers don't know. Why do we have to create our own portrait?

It's a puzzle. It is perhaps intended to make us draw our own identikit. Work for it. The many descriptions given the Creature are overwhelmingly sensory adjectives – 'hideous', 'ugly', 'vile', 'horrid' – describing what Victor feels, not what he sees. As noted elsewhere, there is only one authoritative portrait of the creature; a frontispiece which was either approved, or may even have been advised on, by Mary Shelley. It was commissioned and paid for by the publishers of the 1831 Standard Novel edition,* the last which Mary Shelley saw through the press and for which she was paid the last money she would get for the novel in her lifetime. A measly £30.† One suspects the artist, who was famous, got more.

The frontispiece to the 1831 edition was by Theodore von Holst, an outstanding illustrator of romantic literature. A disciple of Henry Fuseli (with whom Mary's mother had

---

* The Standard Novels, introduced by the publishers Colburn and Bentley, were cheap (six shilling) reprints. They are seen, historically, as precursors of the 20th-century paperback.

† See below, page 231.

once been madly in love), and like him a connoisseur of the ghoulish, it is clear that von Holst read *Frankenstein* attentively. He entered into the spirit of the work – although detail was circumscribed by the small octavo page of the Standard Novels. His picture has been given an enlightening analysis by Ian Haywood, which I gratefully draw on.*

Von Holst's frontispiece illustration, accompanied in the 1831 edition with the quotation: 'By the glimmer of the half-extinguished light, I saw the dull, yellow eye of the creature open; it breathed hard, and a convulsive agitation seized its limbs ... I rushed out of the room.'

....
* See https://romanticillustrationnetwork.wordpress.com/2016/11/26/
image-of-the-month-theodore-von-holst-frankenstein-1831/

There are, Haywood points out, informative features. For example the 'horn-like' electrodes on the left-hand side – attached, one assumes, to out-of-sight Leyden jars. The text has no indication – apart from the word 'sparks' and a lightning-blasted tree – that the creature is animated by external electricity. If it is, it is not by lightning (apologies to James Whale and Benjamin Franklin) but by Voltaic batteries.

Alessandro Volta (1745–1827), a pioneering physicist and the inventor of the electrical battery, saw his electrical-generating tanks as contradicting Galvani's belief that 'animal' electricity was 'life force'. Pump volts into a dead frog's limbs – or a whole corpse, whether whole or patchwork – and it will jerk. But the body, Volta contended, is no more 'alive' than a light bulb when you turn on the switch. The presence of batteries (visual in the picture, implied in the text) deny vitalism and vindicate materialism (see discussion on pages 44–5).* Von Holst guessed, correctly, this was the side Mary Shelley was backing in *Frankenstein*.

In the foreground is Victor's notebook which, in his haste to flee, he has left behind. We later learn that the Creature takes the notes with him when he flees, not, at that point, knowing what it contains. Why is it bound? So that it will be invisible when secreted with other bound books in the bookcase at the back of the room.

The mysterious shaft of light, one notes, is coming not from the cathedral-like window (it's a November night,

* See Richard C. Sha, 'Volta's Battery, Animal Electricity, and *Frankenstein*', https://www.tandfonline.com/doi/abs/10.1080/10509585.2012.639182

Halloween is hinted) but from that bookcase. It metaphoric-
ally signals where Victor has learned the process: like Dr Faust,
from ancient writings as well as surgical dissection (see the
entrails in the foreground). What's the last thing Faust says,
trying, vainly, to propitiate the Devil? 'I'll burn my books.'

One can quote Haywood at some length here:

> The expanding beam of illumination is one of
> the scene's most conspicuous tropes as it has no
> logical function, contradicting the epigraph's 'half-
> extinguished light' and the text's mention of a moon
> that 'struggled' to pierce the gloom. By adding this *fiat
> lux*, Holst reinforced the scene's (and the novel's) trou-
> bling religious and political connotations, as the motif
> is most commonly found in medieval and Renaissance
> representations of the Annunciation ... Holst's shaft
> of light also falls on the creature's cocked left arm,
> which was a pose used in both sculpture and painting
> to represent sleeping beauty, as in Titian's painting *The
> Bacchanal of the Andrians* (1523–6) and the Vatican's
> famous Roman statue the *Sleeping Ariadne*.

There is also a lot of Hogarth in von Holst's picture. The
last plate of the 'Rake's Progress' (see overleaf) – the rake in
syphilitic hell in Bedlam – is prophetic of von Holst's waking
Creature, about to face his hell.

New science versus ancient, calfbound learning is sig-
nalled everywhere in Victor's filthy workshop. There are bones

Last plate of the 'Rake's Progress', by Hogarth.

lying about. There are entrails in the foreground, allusive to Hogarth's dissection study in the 'Four Stages of Cruelty'.

What is most striking, however, is that the creature is, facially and with the Apollonian proportions of his body, handsome. But for how long? The right leg – 'bristled' looking – is evidently decaying, congenitally, into something less baby-smooth. 'Shrivelled' is the term Victor uses.

Victor's short cloak (or is it the student's 'bum-freezer' gown) and appalled face suggests that he is running out of the building. But on his way down, half-fainting (as always), he stops in his room, where he falls into a sleep and has a nightmare about kissing his dead mother. One does not have to be a devotee of Freud to see that Victor Frankenstein's troubles have only begun.

Frankenstein's brain

∞ઠ∾

The body part which raises most curiosity in humans is the brain. It contains what is essentially us. Is the Creature's organ new or stolen? If new, will it grow? And how? If stolen, does it have traces of its previous owner?

The scientist owner of the most famous dead brain in the world shares half a name with the most famous fictional scientist: Einstein/Frankenstein. They share something else besides: stolen brains.

Albert Einstein died, an eminent member of Princeton University, on 18 April 1955. He was 76 years old and the given cause of death was aneurysm. Brian Burrell, in his 2005 book *Postcards from the Brain Museum*, records that 'Einstein had left behind specific instructions regarding his remains: cremate them, and scatter the ashes secretly in order to discourage idolaters'.

Despite this ban, the pathologist on call at Princeton, Thomas Harvey, stole the organ, later protesting he did so for science – a priority which outweighed the owner's mere wishes.* The weighed brain came in at 1,230g (2.7lbs). Weighing dead brains, while still warm, was a practice which went back

* He also removed Einstein's eyes, and gave them to his friend Henry Abrams, Einstein's ophthalmologist.

a century or more. The organ was regarded as the seat of personality and, for the devout, the locus of the soul. We know, for example, that Byron – one of the first auditors of *Frankenstein* – had a five-pounder. Two Einsteins. Make of that what you will.

The brain was an active topic in human biology when Mary was writing. She may well have caught wind of Charles Bell's *Idea for a New Anatomy of the Brain* (1811). Bell claimed to have discovered the key distinction between sensory and motor nerves. The Creature's motor ability is phenomenal. He could sweep the board of Olympic track running, throwing, jumping, and swimming events and still have the energy for a jog. But his senses are strangely numb. He does not, for example, feel cold.

Returning to Einstein, Virginia Hughes tells us that

Harvey soon lost his job at the Princeton hospital and took the brain to Philadelphia, where it was carved into 240 pieces and preserved in celloidin, a hard and rubbery form of cellulose. He divvied up the pieces into two jars and stored them in his basement.*

'Stored' flatters what he did. Over the years Einstein's bottled organ was secreted in various hiding places (beer coolers at one point) until Harvey lost his medical licence in 1988. He became a lowly factory worker and a neighbour of William

---

* http://phenomena.nationalgeographic.com/2014/04/21/the-tragic-story -of-how-einsteins-brain-was-stolen-and-wasnt-even-special/

Burroughs, author of *Naked Lunch* (possibly the most visceral novel ever written):

> The two men routinely met for drinks on Burroughs's front porch. Harvey would tell stories about the brain, about cutting off chunks to send to researchers around the world. Burroughs, in turn, would boast to visitors that he could have a piece of Einstein any time he wanted.

Strange are the ways of science and literature.

There is only one mention of the word 'brain' in Mary Shelley's text – passingly, in the description of Victor's post-operative nightmare:

> I beheld the corruption of death succeed to the bloom-ing cheek of life; I saw how the worm inherited the wonders of the eye and brain.

How Victor came by, or stole, the Creature's unwormed brain is never divulged. Does he transplant a whole head, or does he pour a semi-liquid brain into an alien skull? The fact that the newborn Creature has a mane of flowing black hair suggests a whole head has been transplanted.* We just don't know.

Edward Trelawny recalls that Byron liked to drink from skulls and that, at the incineration of Shelley (where both he

* The luxuriant head of hair was reportedly suggested by Percy, a man proud of his own locks.

and Byron were present) he (Trelawny) took pains to smash Shelley's skull to prevent Byron purloining it for that purpose. In the von Holst illustration there are no fewer than five skulls – all entire – in Victor's 'workshop of filthy creation'.

Film-makers are inventive when faced with Mary Shelley's reticence. In James Whale's *Frankenstein* the doltish Fritz is dispatched to steal a superior brain from the university anatomy department. He clumsily drops the desired organ, smashing the jar. He then guiltily selects an 'abnormal brain' instead (oddly, Victor does not read the label on the jar brought him). It's a scene which sticks in the audience's mind. Mel Brooks plays it up hilariously in *Young Frankenstein*. In the best of the Hammer follow-ups, *The Curse of Frankenstein*, the whole plot revolves around the stolen brain: should it be a hanged murderer's or eminent living professor's? If the latter, how to purloin it?

Kenneth Branagh's *Mary Shelley's Frankenstein* twists the source plot so that the brain is that of the cleverest of Ingolstadt University's scientists, the recently deceased Waldman. He it is who in the novel drags Victor into 1790s *Wissenschaft*, blowing away the young man's misty Paracelsian nonsense:

> 'I am happy,' said M. Waldman, 'to have gained a disciple; and if your application equals your ability, I have no doubt of your success. Chemistry is that branch of natural philosophy in which the greatest improvements have been and may be made; it is on that account that I have made it my peculiar study;

but at the same time I have not neglected the other branches of science. A man would make but a very sorry chemist, if he attended to that department of human knowledge alone. If your wish is to become really a man of science, and not merely a petty experimentalist, I should advise you to apply to every branch of natural philosophy, including mathematics.'

What about the Creature's brain once it has been inserted and is firing on all cylinders? Why is the Creature's consciousness a tabula rasa? Why does he have to learn languages from scratch? He has instincts and appetites, but no memory. Those vaults in his large head are empty.

Mary Shelley poses these cerebral puzzles cunningly and implies answers. She is a materialist, not a vitalist (see pages 44–5) – in this she was four-square with her friend, William Lawrence. The brain, materialists like them maintained, is an organ, nothing more: not the site of the soul or some immaterial 'mind'. It exudes thought as the bladder exudes urine.

Does the Creature have a pre-owned full-size brain? Yes – but it brings nothing with it but brain function. The Creature has to learn the three languages he knows, and skills. There is something in his mixture which makes him, in his first two years of life, brainier than any child prodigy. Harriet Martineau read *Paradise Lost* at six: the Creature does it at one.

On this matter, as on a number of others, Mary Shelley leaves it to the reader to fill in the holes she leaves, like narrative traps. Oddly, it works.

Does the Creature have a penis?

༄༅

It may seem as pointless a question as whether, after living alone, the Creature has a beard, or whether he cuts his toenails with his right or left hand. But, once thought about, the question has serious implications in the story.

It seems trivial – prurient even. But the penis issue, which jocularly (and sometimes vulgarly) obsesses web chat about the novel, has thought-provoking aspects. As Frank Kermode observes, reviewing a very learned book for a very learned journal:

> There is an immemorial taboo on the topic of the sexuality of Jesus, but it has sometimes been defied. Steinberg demonstrates that from about 1260, painters (perhaps affected by the success of the Franciscans, who had a slogan *nudus nudum Christum sequi*) departed from the hieratically clothed, unsexed Byzantine tradition, and undressed the infant Jesus. Thereafter, for two centuries, they pictured him naked but without genital emphasis. But by the end of the 15th century they not only painted his penis but represented it as 'pointed to, garlanded, celebrated', stared at and venerated. In the following century it

was touched and manipulated, and by the 1530s it was sometimes being shown in a state of infantile erection. This theme of erection, though under cover of a loincloth or other garment, was repeated in pictures of the Crucifixion and the dead Christ. There are some extremely fantasticated loincloths in paintings of the Man of Sorrows, as in two 'deeply shocking' pictures by Ludwig Krug (c. 1520) and Maerten van Heemskerck (1532) ... Some renderings of Crucifixion and Pietà are, I think one must agree, clearly intended to suggest large erections, which may have been intended to symbolise Resurrection.*

Certainly D.H. Lawrence believed the resurrection was symbolised in the male groin. *The Man Who Died*, one of his last novellas, also bawdily entitled 'The Escaped Cock' (written around the same time as taboo-flouting *Lady Chatterley's Lover*) has a Jesus who has survived the cross without anyone knowing. He is carnal, a 'man' at last, and has his first sexual congress with a priestess of Osiris. At the moment of climax:

> He crouched to her, and he felt the blaze of his manhood and his power rise up in his loins, magnificent.
> 'I am risen!'

....

* Kermode is reviewing *The Sexuality of Christ in Renaissance Art and in Modern Oblivion* by Leo Steinberg, in the *LRB*, January 1997.

You won't find it in the gospels. Nor in *Frankenstein*. But one wonders. Clearly, when reading the gospels, Lawrence wondered.

There is, as Kermode says, chronic *pudeur* on the subject. There's a relevant moment in the film *Terminator 2* (1991). The android from the future, played by Arnold Schwarzenegger, is one of the many sons of Frankenstein – with a Karloff hairstyle to remind us. He goes into a bar, naked – stripped to the buff for his time travel – to clothe himself in Hell's Angel gear and mobilise himself on one of the Harley-Davidsons outside. The bar girls snatch impressed glances at what the audience will never see.

Did Mary Shelley conceive a monster sans genitalia – like the Lion King, the Incredible Hulk, or King Kong? Or should we picture some kind of fig-leaving, as in *T2*? There is one memorable film adaptation which blasts through this puzzle: Mel Brooks's *Young Frankenstein*, which has a running joke about the Monster's 'enormous schwanz-stucker'.

The bawdy undercurrent raised to comic art by Brooks runs unstoppably elsewhere. The web is rife with speculation about Frankenstein's monstrous genitalia. 'A Frankenstein penis' in urban slang, for example, is 'a penis that has been enlarged to unnatural sizes through the use of various devices and medications'.

Is, then, the Creature, as Mary Shelley devised him, sexual or asexual? Clearly, the evidence of the text suggests, sexual – although the novel does not stress the fact. When he comes upon William, Victor's brother, an uncommonly pretty boy,

the Creature invites him to be his companion. There is something creepy in the request. William spurns the offer with
insult against the 'ogre', 'ugly wretch'. Unable to restrain
himself, the monster strangles the lad – there is recurrently
something carnal in his murders, flesh hands against flesh
throat, an embrace gone wrong. Given his strength he could
kill with a single backhand blow or snap a child's neck like a
celery stalk.

Round the boy's bruised neck the Creature finds a neck-
lace. It has a locketed portrait of a beautiful woman: William's
and Victor's dead mother. The Creature keeps the miniature,
as a sexual fetish. It excites him. He does not know why – he
cannot yet explain these urges, as the description of what he
feels after throttling luckless William makes clear:

> As I fixed my eyes on the child, I saw something glitter-
> ing on his breast. I took it; it was a portrait of a most
> lovely woman. In spite of my malignity, it softened
> and attracted me. For a few moments I gazed with
> delight on her dark eyes, fringed by deep lashes, and
> her lovely lips.

'Delight'?

Soon after, he comes on Justine, the Frankenstein family's
beloved servant, sleeping in the haybarn.* She has been vainly

---

* Mary would have known, by reputation at least, the Marquis de Sade's
notorious 1791 pornographic novel, *Justine; Or, the Misfortunes of Virtue*. In
1816 it had become as loaded a name as 'Lolita' has today.

looking for the lost boy, whom the Creature has strangled. He later recalls the episode for Victor:

I left the spot where I had committed the murder, and seeking a more secluded hiding-place, I entered a barn which had appeared to me to be empty. A woman was sleeping on some straw; she was young, not indeed so beautiful as her whose portrait I held, but of an agreeable aspect and blooming in the loveliness of youth and health. Here, I thought, is one of those whose joy-imparting smiles are bestowed on all but me. And then I bent over her and whispered, 'Awake, fairest, thy lover is near – he who would give his life but to obtain one look of affection from thine eyes; my beloved, awake!'

The sleeper stirred; a thrill of terror ran through me. Should she indeed awake, and see me, and curse me, and denounce the murderer? Thus would she assuredly act if her darkened eyes opened and she beheld me. The thought was madness; it stirred the fiend within me – not I, but she, shall suffer; the murder I have committed because I am forever robbed of all that she could give me, she shall atone. The crime had its source in her; be hers the punishment! Thanks to the lessons of Felix and the sanguinary laws of man, I had learned now to work mischief. I bent over her and placed the portrait securely in one of the folds of her dress. She moved again, and I fled.

'Thy lover is near'? He is clearly sexually aroused. He places the portrait in the folds of her dress. How far do his fingers go? Then, frightened of the fearful sexual confusion which overwhelms him, he leaves. These are the preludes to his howl of despair, when his future mate is destroyed, and his vengeful violation of the body of Elizabeth on her bridal bed.

The moral is Godwinian. If society denies outlets for 'normal' sexual urges, they will find abnormal, anti-social, criminal outlets. Why is the Creature a homicidal rapist? Because he has been bent out of shape by a cruel world. Focus on that, not on him, the novel admonishes us.

Why yellow?

༚༝ༀ

A major reason Victor cannot bear to be in the same room as 'his' newborn is the (temporary?) colour of the Creature's skin and eyes. What is it about yellow that so upsets him?

In Chapter 2, Victor tells us when his great mission began – with a vision:

> When I was thirteen years of age, we all went on a party of pleasure to the baths near Thonon; the inclemency of the weather obliged us to remain a day confined to the inn. In this house I chanced to find a volume of the works of Cornelius Agrippa.

It inspires him:

> what glory ... if I could banish disease from the human frame, and render man invulnerable to any but a violent death!

Victor goes to huge efforts four years later to bring his new man (not superman) to birth; but then, in a spasm of postnatal disgust, walks away from his creation. He is resolved to have nothing to do with it.

The passage goes thus:

> With an anxiety that almost amounted to agony, I collected the instruments of life around me, that I might infuse a spark of being into the lifeless thing that lay at my feet. It was already one in the morning; the rain pattered dismally against the panes, and my candle was nearly burnt out, when, by the glimmer of the half-extinguished light, I saw the *dull yellow eye* of the creature open; it breathed hard, and a convulsive motion agitated its limbs.
>
> How can I describe my emotions at this catastrophe, or how delineate the wretch whom with such infinite pains and care I had endeavoured to form? His limbs were in proportion, and I had selected his features as beautiful. Beautiful! Great God! His *yellow skin* scarcely covered the work of muscles and arteries beneath. [my emphasis]

Why, we might ask, are the Creature's skin and eyes yellow?* But also, why is yellow so disgusting that it impels Victor on the spot to give up what is his masterwork? Puzzling indeed. Particularly since his masterwork won't give Victor up. The colour does not usually have nauseating associations – think

---

* A question also addressed in my book *Who Betrays Elizabeth Bennet?* (1999)

Coldplay and Wordsworthian daffodils. Yellow is only mentioned once elsewhere than Chapter 8, neutrally describing the moon.

One explanation plumps for racial implication. As in the later 19th-century phrase of M.P. Shiel (a disciple of Mary Shelley) the fabled 'Yellow Peril' comes to mind. The interpretation is bolstered by the description of Victor being 'white' in death and Walton's description on first seeing the Creature as 'not European'. Jess Nevins writes that:

> To the 19th century readers of *Frankenstein*, a yellow-skinned, clean-shaven man with long black hair and dun-colored eyes who crosses the steppes of Russia and Tartary would be instantly recognizable as a Mongolian.*

'Instantly' is a stretch. But 'Mongol', then as now, contained overtones. They were, like Genghis Khan, ruthless and savage. Had they not destroyed Rome and its civilisation? There is, Jess Nevins suggests, a legacy if only we open our eyes to it:

> Although Mary Shelley's linkage of the Monster with the Mongols has diminished in the public imagination with the passing of time, the association was a deliberate one on Mary Shelley's part, and the Monster's role as a precursor to the Yellow Peril, cannot be

* Jess Nevins, https://beyondvictoriana.com/2011/05/11/quaint-18-roots-of-the-yellow-peril-part-i/

understated. The Monster was the first image of a Mongol in popular culture which portrayed an Asian not as a small figure but as a large one. The image of a large, dangerous Asian remained in British and American popular culture, becoming one of the motifs of the Yellow Peril.

It explains but does not entirely convince.

To repeat the point, yellow does not normally have negative connotation (as does, for example, 'black'). There is one exception: the association with jaundice. As Dr Google, ever at hand, tells us:

> Jaundice is a common and usually harmless condition in newborn babies that causes yellowing of the skin and the whites of the eyes. The medical term for jaundice in babies is neonatal jaundice. ... The symptoms of newborn jaundice usually develop two to three days after the birth and tend to get better without treatment by the time the baby is about two weeks old.*

Victor Frankenstein does not stick around even two or three minutes but rushes out of the door for good. Not for him a yellow superman. He is, says Anne Mellor, a 'bad mother'.

....
* https://www.nhs.uk/conditions/jaundice-newborn. My friend Jonathan Grossman, a professor at UCLA, was, I believe, among the first to make the link with postnatal jaundice.

Mary Godwin/Shelley was no stranger to the trials and tribulations of childbirth. It has been speculated that her first child, the prematurely born Clara, may have died of jaundice.

On the whole, neo-natal jaundice is more convincing than the Yellow Peril. A clincher, some may think, is that after his birth the Creature is never again described as yellow. Perilous, yes.

There is one last hypothesis. One of the phenomena in the skin of the dying – not yet dead – is that the skin takes on a 'waxen or yellow hue'. Many authorities attest to this discolouration in the last hours of life. It raises the grisly speculation that Victor did not do his harvesting among the dead and buried but those simply at the point of death – he may have stolen living bodies. Sped them on their way, even. A spasm of self-disgust, or the mistaken belief that his creature is dying, leaving him with an eight-foot corpse in his study, may explain his panic-stricken flight downstairs to work out what to do before morning.

Creature 2.0

ঝ৳

Victor Frankenstein makes two Creatures: one at Ingolstadt; the second, four years later, in the Orkneys. How does the creation procedure vary?

Under pressure from his Creature, Victor goes on to create – then destroy – a female Creature. A monstrous Eve. 'Oh! my creator', the Creature beseeches his maker, 'make me happy'. Victor almost does, only to make the Creature very unhappy indeed.

The Creature is a pseudo-man made out of human and animal junk. A 'filthy mass' is what Victor sees, when the creature asks him to create a partner (another filthy mass?) to share life so far away in South America that Victor will never hear of them again. Victor takes the cheese on the trap.

The female Creature is a different kettle of fish – or basket of bits. To make her Victor goes to the northernmost Orkney island, Britain's Ultima Thule, as far as you can get without falling off the British rim. Convenience was not the reason. Victor may, as Walton observes, be able to speak fluently accented English but it is unlikely that he knows Gaelic. The Orkneys are famous for their lightning, which may be a factor. The novel does not say.

There are three huts and five persons living on porridge and a few miserable cows on the God-forsaken rocks which Victor takes over as his second workshop of filthy creation. Even filthier, one would guess, than his first. The Orcadians are 'benumbed by want and squalid poverty', eking out a sparse living in their 'desolate and appalling landscape'. More to the point, there are no surgical dissection theatres, abattoirs, graveyards, or charnel houses for hundreds of miles. Where will Victor get his body parts?

In fact, the Orkneys, about which Mary clearly knew no more than a parlour geographical globe could tell a child,* had in the 1790s a population of 25,000 – mostly fishing communities. Her version is a fictional wilderness. Which is clearly what she wanted at this phase of the narrative.

Victor has brought with him, from Perth, little more than carry-on luggage. There are references to his 'instruments' – like Dr Finlay, he has his doctor's bag.

With his instruments, 'chemicals' (presumably) and possibly an alchemical spell or two he contrives to fabricate his second (fem)creature. Out of what? One wonders, fancifully, whether he brought with him a scrap of the original Creature to work from – what modern medicine might call a stem cell. Theologians might imagine a spare rib.

However he does it, Victor suddenly realises near the point of completion that he has done something very wrong. Once

....
* She spent part of her childhood and youth in Glasgow but never, apparently, visited the Orkneys. They were little regarded until Walter Scott popularised the islands in *The Pirate* (1822).

the two creatures breed, forget South America, the human race faces doom. In short time (the Creature does everything fast). Victor destroys 'her'. Meanwhile, of course, he is being watched, unobserved, by 'him'.

Victor then puts the dismembered corpse (was she, too, eight feet tall?) in a 'basket' – easily handled, apparently – takes it out to sea in a small rowing boat, and drops it four miles offshore, loaded down with stones. Why not bury it? It is, in fact, a wise precaution. The creature has been peering, in his habitual peeping-Tom way, through the hut window, and may now, instructed by Frankenstein's notes and what he observes, be able to perform the animating trick himself. That must never happen.

With what he now knows, the Creature, phenomenally intelligent, might exhume any buried bodily remains and stitch them together as his maker stitched him together. And what then? A new race of Titans. Beware the Lilliputian Homo sapiens. A more sapient species is on the way. Unless Victor does the right thing – sealing, in the process, his own doom and that of everyone he loves.

Frankenstein's bride visualised

༈

Mary Shelley and James Whale could never meet. But they would have admired each other's Frankensteins. In his second film Whale fills in what Mary Shelley leaves blank.

The making and unmaking of Victor's 'Eve' inspired a movie even better than James Whale's canonical 1931 film adaptation. *The Bride of Frankenstein* (1935), unlike its predecessor is, in its overture, period faithful to Shelley. It opens with Percy and Byron (poor Polidori and Claire are written out) acclaiming Mary Shelley (played by the young Elsa Lanchester) for the tale they have just heard at the Villa Diodati. A storm batters outside.

A ruminative expression crosses Mary's face. She has, she tells the poets, a sequel. It flashes up – written narrative becomes movie. We return to the end scene of the earlier film: Henry Frankenstein (i.e. Victor) has apparently died; the Creature has burned to death in a blazing windmill.*

But now it transpires that the monster (Boris Karloff again) has survived in a wet pit beneath the mill. He emerges,

---

* Whale, a very literary director, obviously picked up the fact that one of the books Mary Godwin read which fed into *Frankenstein* was *Don Quixote*, famous for its windmills.

bent on murderous revenge. Formerly mute, in his pit he has learned a modicum of language.

Henry (here married to Elizabeth) is not quite dead either. He recovers, and renews his scientific explorations under his mentor, the sage Doctor Pretorius, who has discovered how to create an artificial brain (again Whale solves that problem more explicitly than Shelley). They will create a new race of 'Gods and Monsters'. That phrase was used as the title of an applauded 1998 film, investigating the troubled mind of Whale, played by Ian McKellen – tormented as the director was by post-traumatic stress from his First World War experience as a British officer and his gay sexuality. The torment fed, the film implies, into his complex depiction of his (not Shelley's) self-disgusted monster. And to Whale's eventual suicide.

In the 1935 film, via various adventures, the Creature becomes a moral being. His future bride is, like himself in the 1931 film, created in a wild storm – literal Sturm und Drang (und Blitz – lightning again). But the bride, played by Lanchester and strangely beautiful, rejects the ugly Creature who embarks on a vengeful orgy of apocalyptic destruction, destroying himself and his never-to-be mate.

Like other good film adaptations Whale's film joins disjoined parts of Mary Shelley's narrative and extrapolates creatively. It enriches the reader's return to the novel. One dearly wishes she could have seen *Bride of Frankenstein*. Although the perennial error in the title might have vexed her.

Universal Studios (maker of the original *Bride*) planned a remake to be released in February 2019, with Javier Bardem as the Creature and Angelina Jolie as his mate. The director, Bill Condon, described how the film would remould Whale, and more distantly Shelley, for the 21st century. It would turn 'everything on its head'. The absent female in traditional *Frankensteins* would be corrected for a less patriarchal age:

> This is Eve before Adam; the bride comes first. So in its own way – you know, we all know the Bride only exists for 10 minutes in the Whale movie. She's there and the movie's over. So I keep thinking [my film is], in a way, at least a tribute to what Whale might have done if he'd made a third Frankenstein movie and he'd done it in the 21st Century.

Alas, this Frankenstein for our time has been 'postponed'.

Was Mary Shelley
a resurrectionist?

გოი

F*rankenstein* is a narrative about what you can do with body parts. Mary Shelley had one body part which, atheist that she was, she revered as a holy relic.

Percy Bysshe Shelley was cremated on the seashore at Viareggio – a famous literary tableau. Because the body was, officially, an immigrant, having washed up after ten days in the Gulf of Spezia, it would otherwise have been subject to quarantine regulations for a period and, most horribly for those who loved him, could have ended up undergoing foren-sic dissection.

Edward ('Captain') Trelawny wrote the event up. He also smashed Shelley's skull as it glowed in the pyre – aware, as has been said, of his fellow mourner Byron's love of drinking wine from skulls. Especially those with a story behind them. Shelley's cranial goblet would have added zest to the lord's wine – the young man, after all, was a proclaimed disciple. Hence the name of the boat in which he died: the *Don Juan*, after Byron's most famous poem.

But the heart was not consumed – a phoenix-like fact. Burning his hand, Trelawny plucked it from the flames. It has been suggested the pericardium was calcified into asbestos resistance by Shelley's earlier tuberculosis.

Shelley's ashes were transported to Rome to be buried there in the Protestant Cemetery. An unpeaceful place for a famous atheist to rest, one might think. The tablet over his remains carried the inscription 'Cor Cordium' – heart of hearts.* But his heart was elsewhere. The cardiac relic eventually came into the possession of Mary. She could have interred it with his ashes at the Protestant Cemetery in Rome but chose not to.

It a became, as legend recalls, a vade mecum carried on her person in a silk bag. Trelawny, it is recorded, also passed on to Mary fragments of skull and ashes. Less romantic versions of the story suggest she stored the heart with other mementos.

Did Mary, against every rational fibre in her being, imagine that her husband might be reincarnated? After her death in 1851 the organ was found in her desk, wrapped in pages of *Adonais*, Percy's elegy on the death of Keats:

> Oh, weep for Adonais – he is dead!
> Wake, melancholy Mother, wake and weep!
> Yet wherefore? Quench within their burning bed
> Thy fiery tears, and let thy loud heart keep
> Like his, a mute and uncomplaining sleep;

---

* Algernon Swinburne wrote a late poem, 'Cor Cordium', celebrating what Shelley's 'wonderful and perfect' heart meant for English political liberty and poetry.

Shelley's heart was not 'loud' but it would be, over the thirty years of Mary's nomadic widowhood, much travelled. Upon her death it was passed on to their son and the 75-year-old organ was at last buried with him in 1889.

Anticlimactically, it has been suggested that it may not have been his heart, but his liver, that Mary carried with her all those years.

Why is the Creature so talkative?

☙❧

In the woods outside Ingolstadt, where he spends a year, having run from Victor, the Creature receives not merely education but higher education. He is monstrously gifted and the more dangerous for it – he can achieve more by his tongue than by his prodigious strength of arm.

After he has animated his creature, making a baby without intercourse or the service of woman, Victor is so exhausted he falls into a deep slumber (post-coital, one might call it) riven by sexually horrific nightmares; one is described:

> I thought I saw Elizabeth, in the bloom of health, walking in the streets of Ingolstadt. Delighted and surprised, I embraced her; but as I imprinted the first kiss on her lips, they became livid with the hue of death; her features appeared to change, and I thought that I held the corpse of my dead mother in my arms; a shroud enveloped her form, and I saw the grave-worms crawling in the folds of the flannel. I started from my sleep with horror.

Horror intensifies when he wakes to see that the Creature has pulled open his bed-curtains and is grinning at him. Grinning?

What does it want? Milk? Blood? Water? Inarticulate gurgles come from the thin-lipped mouth.

For most of the stage and screen adaptations which span off from Mary Shelley's novel, that gurgle is as far as the monster will progress in the art of language. He is as dumb as a doorpost in *Presumption*, the trendsetting 1823 play. In the equally trendsetting James Whale 1931 movie, the creature can grunt but is incapable of facial, let alone vocal expression.

Karloff, in the cruellest high heels in Hollywood history, did wonderful things in Whale's movie, but he never had to memorise a script. This aphasia is a drastic departure from the novel in which the creature picks up languages as easily as he plucks berries and uses his acquired linguistic skills as cleverly as he does his formidable strength of arm and fleetness of foot.

After his inarticulate vociferation to Victor, shivering in his bed, the Creature blunders, speechlessly, not knowing where he is, through the town. He is still in William James's 'blooming buzzing confusion'.

Finally, not yet 24 hours old, he staggers into the safety of the forest. For the next few months he will be a feral child. One wonders if Mary knew something about one of the more famous of them, Victor of Aveyron, who came out of the woods in 1800 to amaze the French and test Rousseau's wildly utopian theories of education without school or social imposition. Was 'nature' the best education for a child, as Wordsworth's *The Prelude* maintained?

> One impulse from a vernal wood
> May teach you more of man,
> Of moral evil and of good,
> Than all the sages can.

Mary's novel is firmly Rousseaustic and Wordsworthian. As regards historical fact, the child Victor, the 'wild boy', was wholly animalic. Rousseau and Wordsworth would have wondered if he had been in the right kind of wood.

Among the trees the Creature comes on a hamlet. From the abandoned hovel where he finds shelter nearby, he spies on a family through windows and chinks in log walls. He steals food and repays his victims with wood stacked outside their house (it is now deep midwinter: a cold time of year in Bavaria). No one seems to notice the firewood or the raids on the pantry.

The Creature makes an astounding discovery, as he later recalls to Victor, talking (now aged around two years) in the style of a linguist describing fieldwork:

> I found that these people possessed a method of communicating their experience and feelings to one another by articulate sounds. I perceived that the words they spoke sometimes produced pleasure or pain, smiles or sadness, in the minds and countenances of the hearers. This was indeed a godlike science, and I ardently desired to become acquainted with it. But I was baffled in every attempt I made for this purpose.

> Their pronunciation was quick; and the words they uttered, not having any apparent connexion with visible objects, I was unable to discover any clue by which I could unravel the mystery of their reference. By great application, however, and after having remained during the space of several revolutions of the moon in my hovel, I discovered the names that were given to some of the most familiar objects of discourse: I learned and applied the words fire, milk, bread, and wood. I learned also the names of the cottagers themselves. The youth and his companion had each of them several names, but the old man had only one, which was father. The girl was called sister, or Agatha; and the youth Felix, brother, or son. I cannot describe the delight I felt when I learned the ideas appropriated to each of these sounds, and was able to pronounce them. I distinguished several other words, without being able as yet to understand or apply them; such as good, dearest, unhappy. I spent the winter in this manner.

He's come a long way in a short time from grunt and gurgle.

The Creature has acquired basic language as the growing baby does and by the same baby steps – first nouns, then family relationship words (mama/dadda), then concepts (mama loves dadda). Except of course he has no mama and dadda. Victor, who assumed ('stole', feminist critics say) both roles, has abandoned him at birth, as babies were left in London on the doorstep of Coram's Foundling Hospital.

What the Creature describes, as every mother (the child's first teacher) will know, is how language is first learned. One remembers that in the years she was writing up *Frankenstein*, Mary Shelley had a newborn child. She probably spent as much time crooning and talking to it as she did on the manuscript she was bringing to birth. A supremely intelligent woman, she knew at first hand as much as Jean Piaget, author of the classic *The Language and Thought of the Child* (1926) could have told her.

The Creature's range of linguistic competence expands when, still doing his peeping Tommery, he eavesdrops and spies on Safie, the Turkish woman who comes to stay with the De Lacy family in their forest cottage. Arabic is her first language; she is being taught European languages by Felix. One can deduce that the Creature too becomes multilingual, with German as his first language.

His multiple verbal skills are important to the plot because in a year's time he is going to traverse the whole of Europe. You can't do that with grunts alone. Particularly without money in your pocket and, to boot, clad in a grimy cloak and no underwear.

As winter gives way to spring in the first year of his life, the Creature already has a power of speech beyond that of most humans. The rudiments of reading and writing, the next phase in his education, he picks up from watching Felix teach his beloved sister Agatha. He also picks up some useful things about love, which he stores away; his sexuality is advancing as fast as his mind. It is strange that no one around the small hamlet notices a giant, of uncouth appearance, peeping through windows and walls and humping vast heaps of wood all over the place.

Like a dog, every human year of life is, for the Creature, seven. Or more. He is ready now for higher education. Improbably, he still has the 'dress' he picked up to cover his nakedness in his scrambled departure from Victor's workshop. Miraculously, one might think, he comes on an abandoned satchel in the woods which contains three books: *Paradise Lost*, *Plutarch's Lives*, and *The Sorrows of Young Werther*, 'written in the language, the elements of which I had acquired at the cottage'.

Paradise Lost is the most important – hence its being cited on *Frankenstein*'s title page. With no experience of the larger world of books, the creature takes Milton's epic to be literal truth. Why has he not happened on a copy of the Bible? There must have been Lutheran bibles, in German, prominently around the habitations he is spying on; not to mention prayers and devotional readings.

When he finally leaves the forest the Creature is not merely verbal and literate but (within his narrow syllabus) intensely well read. At one point, Victor spurns him as 'a filthy mass that moves and talks'. Filthy he may be. There is no reference to his washing or shaving himself and one does not want to think about sanitary arrangements below that vast waist. But the Creature is, as Peter Brooks points out, 'the most eloquent creature in the novel', a master of language – an 'epistomophile' is the word Brooks coins.

The Creature is not what Matthew Arnold would call a 'scholar gipsy', one for whom what he learns is sufficient of itself and the woods all the world he needs. The Creature uses his rhetorical power to master others in the outside world. As noted previously (page 87), at various times he compares himself to Adam (whose first act is linguistic, to name the animals in Eden) and elsewhere Satan – the ex-angel who seduces the mother of mankind, bringing about the downfall of the human race, by speech alone. It is by 'weaponised' language, not force, that the Creature persuades Victor, wholly against his better judgement, to make him a mate.

The Creature can get what he most wants by words. The dying Victor warns his new best friend, Walton, that should he perchance confront the monster to beware what comes out of his mouth. He is diabolically 'eloquent and persuasive'.

So it turns out. When he finds the Creature in the dead Victor's cabin Walton does not (as captain he will have a firearm) blast the monster into kingdom come. He allows himself to be lured into discussion about ethics. Verbally, almost hypnotically, the monster proceeds to run rings round Walton with sophistical Godwinian argument along the lines of: 'I am what you humans have made me. Do not blame me for your friend's death, blame yourself, you human.' And, with words to that effect, he leaps through the cabin window with a Wertherian 'Farewell!' on his way to a Wertherian suicide.*

....
* See below, page 140.

But, in addition to being a master of rhetoric the Creature, like Satan, is a master of lies. Even at the end, as he protests Miltonically, evil is his good. He may have other plans than self-destruction. He is, after all, a frost giant (see page 37). His fiery death is never described – as it well could be (Walton, telescope in hand, might see a distant blaze). The Creature's protestation of imminent suicide may be theatrical: he does not want more expeditions like Walton's coming after him. Mary Shelley artfully leaves a large question mark hanging over the end, which is no clear end, of her story.*

---

* One has to wonder whether she had a sequel in mind and whether, had the original three-volume edition sold better, she might not have produced one.

Le monstre, c'est moi

ᘒᕲᕷ

How much of her own route to learning was Mary Godwin putting into the Creature's woodland education?

Books are my university, said Gogol. They are certainly the Creature's only access to higher learning. He doesn't get to university – except for the one day he comes into the world in Victor's study.

Neither did Mary Godwin attend university. William Godwin's house, the Polygon, was her first seat of learning, and peripatetic travels with Percy Shelley her second. And books, of course: something with which her life was always surrounded.

She read voraciously over the period 1814–17, as her journal testifies. In fact one wonders how she did anything other than read. But she found time for adultery, elopement, bearing children, losing children, foreign travel and keeping grandees like Byron from getting bored.

How the Creature comes by his books is a fuzzy episode. When he surfaces into consciousness among the filth in Victor's workshop he rises and feels Adamic shame about his body. He snatches some 'dress' left by Victor to cover his nakedness. In the clothing (not exactly described) are Victor's handwritten journal and scientific working notes. They record the secret animation process and also, in the domestic entries, throw open a window on to the life, mind and soul of the Creature's creator. The Creature will in time find that information useful.

In the forest where he takes refuge he pries on unwitting households (repaying what they teach him with firewood – a nice Promethean touch). Then a momentous thing happens. He later tells Victor (whose neglected parental responsibility it was to teach his creature how to speak and read) how he came by the printed word:

> One night, during my accustomed visit to the neighbouring wood, where I collected my own food, and brought home firing for my protectors, I found on the ground a leathern portmanteau, containing several articles of dress and some books. I eagerly seized the prize, and returned with it to my hovel. Fortunately the books were written in the language the elements of which I had acquired at the cottage; they consisted of *Paradise Lost*, a volume of *Plutarch's Lives*, and the *Sorrows of Werter*.

He elaborates:

> I can hardly describe to you the effect of these books … In the *Sorrows of Werter*, besides the interest of its simple and affecting story, so many opinions are canvassed, and so many lights thrown upon what had

hitherto been to me obscure subjects, that I found in it a never-ending source of speculation and astonishment ...The disquisitions upon death and suicide were calculated to fill me with wonder.

Goethe wrote *The Sorrows of Young Werther* (1774) when he was in his early twenties. In later life he came to hate his youthful effusion and the indisciplined fever of Sturm und Drang romanticism it chronicles. Too late. It became the most read of his many and varied productions.

Werther, a young man of fashion, loves Charlotte ('Lotte'). But she is promised in marriage to Albert, a rather ordinary fellow. After the wedding, a chagrined Werther borrows Albert's pistols on a pretext. The husband charges his new wife to do the actual handing over. The fact that Lotte has handled the weapons triggers a detonation of fetishised love in Werther:

'They have passed through your hands – you have wiped the dust from them. I kiss them a thousand times – you have touched them. Heavenly Spirits favour my design – and you, Charlotte, offer me the weapon'.

The clock strikes twelve, and with the forlorn cry 'Lotte! Lotte! Farewell! Farewell!' Werther looses a ball into his skull.

Buoyed by the full tide of the German Romantic movement Werther became, for his generation, a hero. The novel inspired a fashion for yellow trousers and, more seriously, an epidemic of copycat suicides – as many as 2,000, it is claimed. The book was banned in Leipzig, Copenhagen, and Milan.

The Creature, in the climax of the novel, is lovelorn. Victor has destroyed the female creature he longed to mate with. Yellow trousers are impossible for legs his size. But suicide can be his grand farewell to a world too cruel for such as him. He does so with an allusive Wertherian echo in his last word 'Farewell!'

'Plutarch', the Creature recalls, 'taught me high thoughts; he elevated me above the wretched sphere of my own reflections, to admire and love the heroes of past ages.' *Paradise Lost* the Creature reads as truth. It is not, for the Creature, allegory or myth, but Revelation. Gospel.

These three 'treasures' constitute what Peter Brooks calls a cyclopaedia universalis. Beware the man of one book, says the proverb. Beware, even more, the man of three. They form a classic university tripos: romantic love, world history, theology.

Later the Creature eavesdrops on Felix instructing Safie with extracts from Volney's *Ruins of Empires*.

> He had chosen this work, he said, because the declamatory style was framed in imitation of the eastern authors. Through this work I obtained a cursory knowledge of history, and a view of the several empires at present existing in the world; it gave me an insight into the manners, governments, and religions of the different nations of the earth. I heard of the slothful Asiatics; of the stupendous genius and mental

activity of the Grecians; of the wars and wonderful
virtue of the early Romans – of their subsequent
degeneration – of the decline of that mighty empire;
of chivalry, Christianity, and kings. I heard of the discovery of the American hemisphere, and wept with
Safie over the hapless fate of its original inhabitants.

The creature sympathises with the genocidally exterminated
Native Americans. He, like them, will suffer a kind of specie-
cide. He, to adapt James Fenimore Cooper's title, is the Last of
the Monsters.

The books are, one might pause to think, a very strange
thing to find, left, in the woods, by some unknown owner. Why
would one go there to read Plutarch? The Creature's rapid evolution from burbling to high-flown literary comprehension – in
a few weeks – similarly strains credulity. But, of course, Mary
Shelley is not talking about him, she is talking about herself
and the crash course of reading Shelley imposed on her after
they declared their love for each other over her mother's grave.
'C'est moi,' Gustave Flaubert said about Madame Bovary. Mary
could have said the same about the educated monster.

Percy gave Mary a copy of *Paradise Lost* to read in June
1815, exactly one year before the Villa Diodati party. She studied and read it several times prior to writing *Frankenstein*, her
journal records.

The Creature makes clear to Victor that he has read these
books 'in the language the elements of which I had acquired
at the cottage'. The Germanising of *Paradise Lost* was a highly

contested issue in Switzerland – where *Frankenstein* the novel came into being. Johann Jakob Bodmer, a Swiss professor of Helvetian history at the University of Zurich had translated Milton's epic in 1732. It was promptly excoriated and banned for falsifying the Bible. The rebellious God-defying Adam, celebrated by quotation on Mary Shelley's title page was a principal offence.

As Adam Foley tells us:

> It can be said without exaggeration that the German-Swiss writer's life's work was the translation, defense and dissemination of Milton's *Paradise Lost* for the first time among a wide German readership. From 1732 to 1780, Bodmer published no less than six different German translations of the epic.*

It must, we can speculate, be one of the later versions that the Creature comes across in 1790. Bodmer, Foley goes on to say, made *Paradise Lost* 'one of the chief agents in the transition between the German *Aufklärung*, or Enlightenment, and Romanticism'. In its way, the radically Miltonic *Frankenstein* was another small bridge between the 18th- and 19th-century movements.

Mary Shelley studied *Plutarch's Lives* in 1815, her journal reveals; with, doubtless, the lofty response the Creature describes. Over the same period she read *Werther* several times.

....

* Adam Foley, http://airshipdaily.com/blog/08122014-paradise-lost-europe

Goethe's book spoke to her personally. Her mother had tried, like Werther, to kill herself for unhappy love. In his memoir of her, Godwin went so far as to call Wollstonecraft a 'female Werther'. Mary herself may have considered suicide in the scandal and stress of running away. There was, as has been said, a lot of suicide around the Shelley–Byron circle at the time.

Constantin François Chasseboeuf, comte de Volney's *The Ruins; Or, a Survey of the Revolutions of Empires* (1792) had also become part of Mary Shelley's intellectual fabric when she was writing *Frankenstein*. Only Walton, in later life, could have survived to read it by the novel's internal chronology. One of William Godwin's friends, James Marshall, translated it.

Volney's *Ruins* was a major political influence on Shelley's 1813 political poem *Queen Mab*. One can imagine him 'instructing' Mary (like Felix instructing Agatha) about it over the tomb of her mother. Volney is the only – indirect – reference in *Frankenstein* to the then currently raging French Revolution; he was one of its intellectual architects and theorisers.

In short, Mary Godwin, later Mary Shelley, read a life-changing amount between 1814 and 1817.* She never went to university but, like Gogol, she didn't need to.

----

* See *The Journals of Mary Shelley, 1814–1844* (1987), Paula R. Feldman and Diana Scott-Kilvert (eds).

A vegan monster?

～❧～

The Creature, unlike other babies, has to feed himself when, on the run, he makes it to the woods. His chosen diet is 'natural'.

One of the many strands woven into *Frankenstein* is a vegetarian tract, expounding dietary politics. It is a strange place to find assertions about healthy eating and animal rights. The question is: does the novel carry it comfortably or does it, in places, sink under the weight of this extraneous cargo. And does it successfully argue its rightness?

Mary Shelley knew all about vegetarianism – in her day called the Pythagorean system. The v-word did not appear in popular discourse until 1840s and its offshoot was not defined until the Vegan Society proclaimed it in their manifesto in 1979. I'll use both terms here.

In 1804, when she was seven, Mary's father imposed the Pythagorean menu on his family. He justified it as rationality in the kitchen (he was not so rational, of course, as to cook his own food). In late adolescence Mary and Percy, a recent convert to 'natural' diet, were kindred spirits on the topic of eating. The meetings over Mary Wollstonecraft's tomb were not hearty picnics, we apprehend.

Percy's views on the ethical rightness, political correctness, health benefits and social virtue of avoiding meat – which he believed was, among other things, a source of syphilis and an instigation to war – were expressed in a fiery pamphlet spun off in 1813 from his political poem *Queen Mab*. The polemic was called *A Vindication of Natural Diet*.

Percy's diet, throughout his life, was a notch beyond natural, verging on the eccentric. 'The Percy Bysshe Shelley Cookbook' would be even thinner than the *Vindication*'s 43 pages. As the pamphlet's title suggests Shelley was strongly influenced in his eating choices by his close friend the radical vegetarian John Frank Newton, author of *The Return to Nature; Or, a Defence of the Vegetable Regimen* (1811).

Shelley's university friend Jefferson Hogg describes a meal at the Newtons' table at which he was a somewhat unenthusiastic guest:

Certainly their vegetable dinners were delightful. Flesh never appeared; nor eggs bodily in their individual capacity, nor butter in the gross: the two latter were admitted into cookery, but as sparingly as possible, under protest, as culinary aids not approved of, and soon to be dispensed with. Cheese was under the ban. Milk and cream might not be taken unreservedly; however, they were allowed in puddings, and to be poured sparingly into tea, as an indulgence to the weakness of neophytes.

Alcohol was also under the ban – even the wholesome, all-English tipple of Hogarth's Beer Street.

Newton's return to prelapsarian Nature involved, in addition to the vegetable regimen, universal nudism, called at the time 'nakedism'. By eschewing flesh on the table and garb on the loins it would be possible to recover pristine noble savagery. As for bodily covering, Newton theorised that it had been enforced on mankind not by sin (as Genesis chronicled, setting God to work with His needle and thread) but by the human species' drift north from the sunny south of the planet. The Newtons, in fact, were a notorious slave-owning family, whose slaves, labouring in their sugar plantations in the West Indian heat, doubtless found it easier to strip off their clothes and be 'natural'. Newton personally was against slavery, but benefited from it.

According to Shelley – who could afford the vastly expensive yacht he spent his final hours in – 'It is only the wealthy that can, to any great degree, even now, indulge the unnatural craving for dead flesh'. As with much else he wrote, this is beautiful nonsense. Fruit and delicate vegetables were high in price and only available to those with cultivated palates and money, while the lower classes ate tripe, pigs' trotters, chitterlings and, on high days and holidays, boiled beef and carrots.

Shelley's views on natural diet feed via Mary into *Frankenstein*. The Creature, newborn, wanders nude (or as good as) through the busy streets of Ingolstadt.* A gigantic nakedist. Finally he makes it to:

....
* See above, page 88.

the forest near Ingolstadt; and here I lay by the side of a brook resting from my fatigue, until I felt tormented by hunger and thirst. This roused me from my nearly dormant state, and I ate some berries which I found hanging on the trees or lying on the ground. I slaked my thirst at the brook, and then lying down, was overcome by sleep.

There cannot be a rich crop of berries in November in Bavaria. Rose hips perhaps. But this, the Creature discovers, is what his body needs, along with roots, fungus and nuts which he later forages.

In his wanderings through the lonely wilderness (now with a cloak keeping the cold off) he finds a fire left by a band of mendicants. 'Some of the offals that the travellers had left had been roasted, and tasted much more savoury than the berries I gathered from the trees.' Most would agree. The 'offals' he nonetheless disdains – meat instinctively displeases. But he tries placing his fruit and veg on the live embers: 'the berries were spoiled by this operation, and the nuts and roots much improved.' Thank you, Prometheus.

These culinary discoveries build up to his tempting offer to Victor later in the story. He will emigrate to the jungles of South America with his mate, if Victor Frankenstein makes him that mate. The civilised world need worry about him no more:

If you consent, neither you nor any other human being shall ever see us again; I will go to the vast wilds of South America. My food is not that of man; I do not destroy the lamb and the kid to glut my appetite; acorns and berries afford me sufficient nourishment. My companion will be of the same nature as myself and will be content with the same fare. We shall make our bed of dried leaves; the sun will shine on us as on man and will ripen our food.

And, under the tropical sun, fruit (perhaps not acorns) will be hanging around them year round; clothes will be superfluous and, as they once were, unnatural. They will, as Newton hypothesised (madly) find the natural state of humanity in the global south.

The image of the lamb is powerful. It is, of course, a traditional symbol of Christ – the saviour eaten ritually as bread or wafer at Mass by the faithful. Can anyone of sensibility look at a lamb (say, Mary's little lamb, fleece as white as snow) then eat it for supper? Shelley enlarges on the question in *Queen Mab*:

> No longer now
> He slays the lamb that looks him in the face,
> And horribly devours his mangled flesh;

So much for Dr Johnson's John Bullish assertion that 'any of us would kill a cow, rather than not have beef'. Or not look a lamb in the face cold-bloodedly if it meant chops that night. Shelley's good-natured friend Thomas Love Peacock (who satirised Percy as Scythrop in *Nightmare Abbey*), observing the poet was sick, mischievously prescribed three lamb chops. Shelley duly did what he was told and improved immensely.

It is clear that what the Creature has in mind when he and his mate get to South America is what the poets Coleridge and Southey called a 'Pantisocracy' – a new Eden in the wilderness. Pre-Fall Eden, as outlined in Genesis and *Paradise Lost*, is a gigantic vegan kitchen, where the primal couple have: 'For dinner savoury fruits, of taste to please'.

Ironically the Creature ends up, mateless, in the icy wastes of the north polar region where there is nothing to eat but meat (seals, penguins, albatrosses) and fish. If you're lucky. Where the polar bears – no Pythagoreans they – will do what they can to eat you. The nearest fruit is three thousand miles south. What does the monster, with his massive metabolic system, sustain himself with in geodetic latitude 90 degrees north?

Shelley was the most outspoken and proselytising of the Romantic vegetarians. But Byron as well 'kept to Pythagoras' and an 'entire vegetable' diet. He did, unlike Shelley, make an exception for alcohol. In 1807 he confessed:

> Apropos, sorry to say, been drunk every day, and not quite sober yet – however, touch no meat, nothing but fish, soup, and vegetables, consequently it does me no harm ...

If only. Byron later gave up fish, restricting himself to dry biscuits and a mess of salad whose contents baffled carnivore acquaintances. Retaining his svelte figure may have been as important to him as dietary politics.

Byron's congenial eating habits at Villa Diodati are recorded with exactitude:

> His system of diet here was regulated by an abstinence almost incredible. A thin slice of bread, with tea, at breakfast – a light, vegetable dinner, with a bottle or two of Seltzer water, tinged with *vin de Grave*, and in the evening, a cup of green tea, without milk or sugar, formed the whole of his sustenance. The pangs of hunger he appeased by privately chewing tobacco and smoking cigars.*

Lenten fare. One wonders whether Polidori's story of the vampire who tears flesh to suck on human blood (no seltzer water for him) was one of the reasons for Byron becoming displeased with the young doctor.

Both Shelleys around the same time were fascinated by the Prometheus myth. Percy was writing *Prometheus Unbound* as *Frankenstein* was published in 1818. As he had explained earlier, in one of the notes to *Queen Mab*:

> The story of Prometheus, is one likewise which, although universally admitted to be allegorical, has never been satisfactorily explained. Prometheus

....
* Thomas Moore, *Life of Lord Byron* (1839).

stole fire from heaven, and was chained for this crime to mount Caucasus, where a vulture continually devoured his liver, that grew to meet its hunger. Hesiod says, that before the time of Prometheus, mankind were exempt from suffering; that they enjoyed a vigorous youth, and that death, when at length it came, approached like sleep, and gently closed their eyes.

Prometheus, (who represents the human race) effected some great change in the condition of his nature, and applied fire to culinary purposes; thus inventing an expedient for screening from his disgust the horrors of the shambles. From this moment his vitals were devoured by the vulture of disease. It consumed his being in every shape of its loathsome and infinite variety, inducing the soul-quelling sinkings of premature and violent death. All vice arose from the ruin of healthful innocence. Tyranny, superstition, commerce, and inequality, were then first known, when reason vainly attempted to guide the wanderings of exacerbated passion. I conclude this part of the subject with an extract from Mr. Newton's *Defence of Vegetable Regimen*, from whom I have borrowed this interpretation of the fable of Prometheus.

The downfall of man? Blame the lamb chop.

Prometheus, the god who gave cookery to mankind, has much to answer for. As Shelley wrote in his *Vindication*:

It is only by softening and disguising dead flesh by culinary preparation that it is rendered susceptible of mastication or digestion, and that the sight of its bloody juices and raw horror does not excite intolerable loathing and disgust.

A further explanation of why Victor (although perhaps a meat eater) found his workshop of creation 'filthy'. Lots of bloody flesh juice there.

One can finish with one of the more odd episodes in Mary Shelley's narrative. The Creature plays cat and mouse with Victor, drawing him ever closer to the North Pole. Victor follows the track meticulously left for him – knowing in his heart that he has no chance of vanquishing the pistol-packing Titan. One clue left by the Creature is perplexing in the extreme:

What his feelings were whom I pursued I cannot know. Sometimes, indeed, he left marks in writing on the barks of the trees or cut in stone that guided me and instigated my fury. 'My reign is not yet over' – these words were legible in one of these inscriptions – 'you live, and my power is complete. Follow me; I seek the everlasting ices of the north, where you will feel the misery of cold and frost, to which I am impassive. You will find near this place, if you follow not too tardily, a dead hare; eat and be refreshed. Come on, my enemy; we have yet to wrestle for our lives, but many

hard and miserable hours must you endure until that
period shall arrive.'

The dead hare is strange. It is of course the fastest of animals
and the Creature is proud of his superior speed. There is a hare
and hounds allusion – catch me if you can, you slow-footed
human hound. But the main point being made is that Victor is
a corrupt meat eater. He, the Creature, needs no dead animal
flesh (which he has nonetheless killed in the shape of the hare)
but can sustain himself, on ice, pure water (only distilled water
could be drunk by Newtonites) and handfuls of nuts he has
presumably brought with him.

Or has the Monster, horrible thought, foregone his vegetarianism? He stole from the Inuits winter 'provisions' together
with his sled and dogs. Neither dogs nor Eskimos (as they were
then called) are great vegetarians. Those provisions, given the
bleak northern latitudes, would be overwhelmingly meat pro-
tein: blubber, dried fish and cured meats. No fruit or pulses
(Percy's preferred sustenance) whatsoever.

As nutrition expert Dr John McDougall tells us, on his
blog:

> Hunted animals, including birds, caribou, seals,
> walrus, polar bears, whales, and fish provided all the
> nutrition for the Eskimos for at least 10 months of
> the year. And in the summer season people gathered a
> few plant foods such as berries, grasses, tubers, roots,
> stems, and seaweeds. Frozen snow-covered lands were

unfit for the cultivation of plants. Animal flesh was, by necessity, the only food available most of the time.*

The last act of *Frankenstein* is played out in Arctic summer. But it's hard to think the scant vegetable provender of the Inuit would keep the Creature's huge physiology going at top speed.

In short, the story ends in vegan hell, as well as all the other hells.

---

* https://www.drmcdougall.com/misc/2015nl/apr/eskimos.htm

Mary Shelley's nautics

୬୧

After Trafalgar the nautical novel enjoyed a long vogue in Britain. *Frankenstein* qualifies in two ways. The polar frame is one. The other nautical subplot is set in the Orkneys where, under pressure, Victor first makes and then destroys the Creature's putative mate. Then takes to the waves. So does the Creature.

Four years after the publication of the first *Frankenstein*, Percy was drowned. In a funeral composed as beautifully as a poem, his body was cremated on the shore where, after ten days in the water, it had been washed up. Present were Byron, Edward Trelawny, and Leigh Hunt. Authors all. Mary did not attend. A volume of Keats's poems was found in Shelley's pocket. The reason for cremation by the edge of the country was less high-literary than may appear. As has been said, his corpse, had it not been burned, would have been, by law, quarantined lest it import communicable disease into Italy.

There are different versions of how the tragedy happened, even from the man who knew the poet well and the ways of the sea best, 'Captain' Trelawny. Richard Holmes gives the comprehensive account.* Shelley, as Holmes records, despite Trelawny's deprecating his seamanship,

....

* In *Shelley: The Pursuit* (1974). I follow Holmes closely and gratefully in what follows.

had considerable previous experience with sailing boats, from schoolboy expeditions up the Thames, to sailing single-handed (or with his ex-Royal Navy friend, Edward Williams) down the Arno, the Serchio, and beyond Livorno harbour out to sea.

He had sailed with Byron, who admired his skill and pluck. The yacht in which Percy was drowned was called, in tribute to the other poet (and perhaps their shared sexual athleticism) *Don Juan*. Byron, celebrator of 'corsairs', had a full-sized schooner, the *Bolivar* – named after the South American revolutionary. A nobler craft. Shelley was chronically aware of being outshone by his friend. During one of his writer's blocks he expressed his sense of inferiority with rueful wit: 'I do not write – I have lived too long near Lord Byron & the sun has extinguished the glow-worm.'

His new yacht (soaking up more of his money than was advisable) was delivered to Shelley in Lerici, Italy in May 1822. He had been, up to this point, as Holmes reminds us, principally a river sailor: 'The Don Juan was his first ocean-going boat', twin-masted, and designed for speed. It carried too much sail for stability. Holmes doubts its seaworthiness: too much had been sacrificed for high performance in calm water.

On 1 July Percy set out on a seven-hour voyage to Livorno to meet Leigh Hunt, staunch friend to the Romantic poets (particularly Keats, recently buried at Livorno). On the return trip Shelley had a crew of three. The vessel, given its extent of sail, was, Holmes judges, undermanned. Particularly when a squall blew up. The wind, poor vessel design and bad luck wrecked the *Don Juan*. Waiting to find out what had happened must have been among the worst days of Mary's life. There were, sadly, many worse days to come.

What is interesting is that a large chunk of *Frankenstein* reverberates with Mary's eerily prophetic fear of this maritime disaster.

To summarise the nautical episode that takes place in the main narrative: Victor has gone to the Orkney Islands, having been harassed and pursued across the face of Europe by the Creature, who demands that the scientist make him a mate. Or else. With her the Creature can found a species as did Adam and Eve, Victor's distant ancestors.

Having all but finished the demanded mate, Victor tears her to shreds. Is she alive, one wonders. Does she experience agony, which would make it a kind of murder? No detail is given. Victor then disposes of the dismembered carcass in the inclement North Sea. He rows far out to do so. The moon fleets from behind skittering clouds. The fragments of the aborted female creature will join the 'slimy things with legs' which so appal Coleridge's ancient mariner.

The Creature, now denied species perpetuity, has witnessed Victor's acts, peering through the Orcadian workshop window. He is infuriated, denied as he is the procreation that even the earthworm can expect. But we feel sympathy with Victor. He has saved the human race from the New Titans who would war against them, as the Old Titans did against the Olympians.

Too exhausted to return to shore, Victor falls unconscious to the boards of his boat. He wakes up some twelve hours later, lying off the coast of Ireland, as he will discover. He improvises a sail out of his clothes, voyaging to port under full shirt power. It is not convincing. It indicates a nautical inexpertise bordering on that of the owl and the pussycat.

Nonetheless, Victor makes land; he knows not where. If there is another clinching reason for supposing Percy did not write *Frankenstein* it is the nautical improbability of this *voyage imaginaire*.

An improbable voyage

❧

The Creature also makes an Orkney to Ireland trip in pursuit of Victor. With evil intent. But how is not clear.

In considering this episode, we might start with another puzzle. What is the point of Clerval in this novel? Henry is referred to as Victor's 'beloved'. He comes to 'love' him, he says, after his friend rescues him at Ingolstadt. Elizabeth, whom according to his mother's deathbed instruction Victor is to marry, matters little to him when it comes to carnal love. Or he to her. She has already written him, when he reaches the age of majority, releasing him from his mother's diktat. They may remain as they have always been: loving brother and sister. 'Beloved' is not the word. With her it is agape not Eros.

Victor does not take advantage of his fiancée's offer to free him but goes ahead, fatefully, with the arranged marriage. Even though the Monster has promised to kill Frau Frankenstein before she merits the title. 'I will be with you on your wedding night.' The promise is repeated no fewer than four times in the novel. What is the difference between that ominous statement and, say, 'I will be at your wedding'? What the Creature means is that he will be in the marital bed when, or before, the virginal couple enjoy, legitimately and at last, each other's bodies.

Victor's outspokenly passionate friendship with Clerval reminds one that Shelley was bisexual – something that Mary surely knew or suspected. One of the other authors spinning yarns at the Villa Diodati most certainly swung both ways, as the whole world was aware.

Byron was actively gay and pederastic up to the moment of his death at Missolonghi. One may suspect his interest in Polidori, handsome young Scot that he was, had an erotic element to it. Five hundred pounds was a goodly salary for an inexperienced physician – grand tour thrown in – and why, anyway, did Byron need a personal physician? Switzerland then, as now, had the best in the world on call.

Clerval's foreground presence in the plot is pointless, unless we allow ourselves the liberty of reading between the lines. By contrast with the scientific-philosophical Victor, Henry is romantic, poetic, and literary. At Ingolstadt it is Henry who tenderly nurses Victor back to health – which means, presumably, washing his unclothed body and seeing to his sanitary needs. Henry has travelled hundreds of miles by stagecoach ostensibly to study at Ingolstadt but in reality to be united with his friend. Henry (is there nothing else in his life?) accompanies Victor on his European trip and then to Scotland. Elizabeth, meanwhile, languishes in Geneva. Waiting for letters that never come.

In Scotland Victor leaves Henry in Perth to go by himself to the windswept Orkneys to make his second Creature. Once he has his mate, the first Creature assures Victor, the couple will emigrate to South America, never to be heard of again in the civilised world. On what vessel two giants without luggage or money, requiring a diet of berries will get passage across the Atlantic is hard to imagine.

Perth, the gateway to the Highlands, is some 200 miles over rough land and rough water from Orkney, the outer rim of Scotland, where Victor assembles and disassembles the future Mrs Monster. What happens after that is one of *Frankenstein*'s more Gordian plot tangles.

The last glimpse of the Monster, after the burial at sea of his prospective mate's body parts, is his speeding off 'like an arrow' in his skiff, in a southerly direction. He has left, as his farewell, his curse about being with Victor on his wedding night – a gruesome *ménage a trois* in prospect. It's a minor puzzle how the Creature has found out about Victor's marriage plans.

Nor is it clear how the Creature is achieving high speed over the choppy waters of the North Sea. As later details make clear, he is making full speed ahead to Perth where Clerval is kicking his heels, waiting for Victor's return.

Perth is a dramatic city – Clerval, we are told, likes to be there because its nearby mountains remind him of the Alps. It is connected to the sea via the River Tay – requiring precise navigation to moor at the port. The Monster locates Clerval (how does he know where he is?) at night and abducts him. This we know because twelve hours later his corpse is still warm. He humps his captive back to his trusty skiff. As usual no one in the populous city, where fishermen rise early, notices a giant stravaging about the streets with a grown man on his back.

The Creature then beats and tacks back against the current nor'-easter to circumnavigate Scotland. Some hundreds of nautical miles. He passes again the outlying Orkneys, where to the best of the Monster's knowledge Victor still is, his obvious next move being to return to his cabin. But, of course, Victor is sleeping in his drifting boat.

The monster apparently overtakes Victor to drop Clerval's body somewhere on the shore of an unnamed coastal town in the east of Ireland. Unlikelihood multiplies. Having made land he finally strangles Clerval, to be found, his body still warm, in a few hours by the authorities. The murderer at this point is unknown to them, although the Creature has left enough clues for Inspector Clouseau to have found him.

Fortuitously, a distraught and wholly disoriented Victor will land, driven by luck, wind and his shirt sail to exactly the same spot in Ireland as did the Monster and his grisly cargo. He did not know exactly what voyage Victor intended – and neither did Victor. He has not sailed but drifted. When he sees Clerval's corpse, Victor collapses. He is duly accused of having murdered his still-warm beloved.

So how did this string of happenstance come about? My assumption is (although it is not made clear by Mary Shelley) that the Monster abducted the living Clerval sometime earlier, having followed the two men to Perth. Given his habit of peeking through bedroom windows, he will know they are the most important persons in each other's lives. His intention was to use the living Clerval in a *Bridge of Spies*-style handover – to prevent Victor reneging on his promise. When he sees the female creature destroyed (again through a window) and dumped at sea he resolves on revenge. Using his preternatural strength, and uncanny nautical skills, he tows the unconscious Victor's rowing boat to Ireland and, with a cunning laying of clues, makes him seem the murderer. Step one in his revenge. Elizabeth is next.

All this is suppositious. What finally puzzles is why, with thirteen years between the first 1818 and the authoritative 1831 editions, Mary did not do some judicious plot repair. It remains a challenge for the reader. I merely offer my solution – others will have more ingenious explanations.

Is Victor a necrophile?

༕

After being cleared of the murder of Clerval, Victor is taken by his father from Ireland back to Geneva, where his marriage with Elizabeth will now go ahead. As promised, the Creature will be there too.

The most blood-chilling episode in *Frankenstein* is that of Victor returning to find Elizabeth, his bride to be but never to be, lain out, scantily robed (we might guess), and strangled across the bridal bed:

> She was there, lifeless and inanimate, thrown across the bed, her head hanging down and her pale and distorted features half covered by her hair. Everywhere I turn I see the same figure – her blood-less arms and relaxed form flung by the murderer on its bridal bier.

'Relaxed' strikes a contradictory note – rigor mortis, eternal unrelaxation, is imminent. The Creature, however, has fulfilled his promise, 'I will be with you on your wedding night'. The word 'night' implied that whatever he had in mind was to occur after the ceremony but before the consummation. It is nine o'clock when Elizabeth screams her last.

The murder occurs in the no man's (literally) land of marriage. Elizabeth is married but still a maiden. So will she die. 'Bier' is a term for the platform on which the coffin is placed. The reader anticipates, of course, the compound 'bridal bed'.

The author has set the scene up lengthily, allowing a slow build to a grisly 'rushed' climax. As the day of the marriage draws near Victor's heart 'sinks', an apprehension he covers with a forced 'appearance of hilarity', for his father's sake.

He carries, unhilariously, pistols (in his bosom) and a dagger.* Even at the ceremony, it seems. Elizabeth projects 'placid content'. She will go to her death knowing nothing of Victor's 'dreadful secret' – he intends, apparently, to tell her later. If need be. Prior knowledge, particularly of his failure to save Justine from the gallows, might have given her second thoughts about marrying Victor Frankenstein.

The atheistical Mary Shelley does not describe the presumably Lutheran 'ceremony' which takes place. Thereafter, the couple are to travel by water to Cologny (where, we recall, the Villa Diodati is), breaking their journey at Evian, where they will spend their first night of marriage. The weather is warm. The lake's waters are clear. Even the looming Mont Blanc seems to smile down at them. 'Those,' says Victor, 'were the last moments of my life during which I enjoyed the feeling of happiness.'

---

* Two pistols because they are one-shot weapons. Victor is taking no chances.

A house has been acquired for the couple's married life near Geneva. What Victor intends to do for a living is not said. They land at sunset and adjourn to an inn:

> The wind, which had hitherto carried us along with amazing rapidity, sank at sunset to a light breeze; the soft air just ruffled the water and caused a pleasant motion among the trees as we approached the shore, from which it wafted the most delightful scent of flowers and hay. The sun sank beneath the horizon as we landed, and as I touched the shore I felt those cares and fears revive which soon were to clasp me and cling to me for ever.

That evening the weather changes – always a portent in the narrative. A storm whips up. A suspicious Victor inspects every corner of their inn 'that might afford a retreat to my adversary'. Elizabeth, meanwhile, prepares herself in the bridal chamber for the ceremonial feast. In white, presumably.

When Victor hears a shrill and dreadful scream he rushes into her room to find her 'lifeless and inanimate' as described above. He recoils in his usual swoon. Afterwards:

> When I recovered I found myself surrounded by the people of the inn; their countenances expressed a breathless terror, but the horror of others appeared only as a mockery, a shadow of the feelings that oppressed me. I escaped from them to the room where

lay the body of Elizabeth, my love, my wife, so lately living, so dear, so worthy. She had been moved from the posture in which I had first beheld her, and now, as she lay, her head upon her arm and a handkerchief thrown across her face and neck, I might have supposed her asleep. I rushed towards her and embraced her with ardour, but the deadly languor and coldness of the limbs told me that what I now held in my arms had ceased to be the Elizabeth whom I had loved and cherished. The murderous mark of the fiend's grasp was on her neck, and the breath had ceased to issue from her lips.

So the 'fiend' is indeed 'with' Victor on his wedding night – he now appears grinning at the window, pointing ironically at the bridal bed/bier and the body of the woman that he has recently molested and killed:

I rushed towards the window, and drawing a pistol from my bosom, fired; but he eluded me, leaped from his station, and running with the swiftness of lightning, plunged into the lake.

It is the second time in as many minutes that Victor has 'rushed'. In the quote above he tells us: 'I rushed towards her and embraced her with ardour'. It could not be explicitly printed in 1818 but one assumes that the creature has not merely strangled, but violated Elizabeth.

The 'ardour' with which Victor embraces her corpse is interesting. One recalls Victor's sexually perverse nightmare, after having looked, in disgust, at what he has made in his filthy workshop in Ingolstadt. It is the only other actual description of any 'ardent' physical encounter in the novel (those between Clerval and Victor, in their months in Germany and years on their grand tour, are implied, not described):

> I slept, indeed, but I was disturbed by the wildest dreams. I thought I saw Elizabeth, in the bloom of health, walking in the streets of Ingolstadt. Delighted and surprised, I embraced her, but as I imprinted the first kiss on her lips, they became livid with the hue of death; her features appeared to change, and I thought that I held the corpse of my dead mother in my arms; a shroud enveloped her form, and I saw the grave-worms crawling in the folds of the flannel. I started from my sleep with horror; a cold dew covered my forehead, my teeth chattered, and every limb became convulsed.

Victor, as Freudian critics have hypothesised, has been psychically deformed by the death of his mother. As James Heffernan points out, the dream and the 'ardent' embrace (on a dead body) are the only occasions Victor is described even touching Elizabeth.*

....

* I am indebted to Professor Heffernan's shrewd analysis of the scene: http://knarf.english.upenn.edu/Articles/hefferna.html

One of the things the major *Frankenstein* films routinely do, drawing on Peake's *Presumption*, is to invent an assistant (often deformed) who does (literally) the 'dirty work'. Fritz in *Presumption* and Whale's *Frankenstein*, Igor in *Young Frankenstein*.

The invented, deformed assistant may be seen as an improvement on what Mary wrote. It stretches credulity to imagine Victor digging up graves himself, breaking by violence into teaching hospitals, abattoirs and charnel houses, night after night over months, then storing the decaying stolen materials, unrefrigerated, over a hot German summer, in a university study, regularly cleaned, presumably, by servants and others who have master keys. It makes more sense for him to work, as films routinely picture, in a secret laboratory with some physically repellent gofer – Victor Frankenstein's Mr Hyde, we may surmise.

But the film's 'improvement' runs directly counter to what Mary Shelley actually wrote:

> I pursued nature to her hiding-places.* Who shall conceive the horrors of my secret toil as I dabbled among the unhallowed damps of the grave or tortured the living animal to animate the lifeless clay? My limbs now tremble, and my eyes swim with the remembrance; but then a resistless and almost frantic impulse urged me forward; I seemed to have lost

---

* Critics have pointed out the significance of 'her' not 'its'.

all soul or sensation but for this one pursuit. It was indeed but a passing trance, that only made me feel with renewed acuteness so soon as, the unnatural stimulus ceasing to operate, I had returned to my old habits. I collected bones from charnel-houses and disturbed, with profane fingers, the tremendous secrets of the human frame. In a solitary chamber, or rather cell, at the top of the house, and separated from all the other apartments by a gallery and staircase, I kept my workshop of filthy creation; my eyeballs were starting from their sockets in attending to the details of my employment. The dissecting room and the slaughter-house furnished many of my materials; and often did my human nature turn with loathing from my occupation, whilst, still urged on by an eagerness which perpetually increased, I brought my work near to a conclusion.

Dirty work it indeed is. And Victor does it himself.

One concludes that Victor Frankenstein is fascinated, sexually fascinated, by dead bodies. It is not dirty work, but dirty thrills, which he gets from physical-sexual contact with the corpse. In answer to the titular question – yes, distinctly necrophile.

Monster or peeping Tom?

ംൽ

At every critical juncture of the novel the Creature is at a window. The last we see of him is jumping in and out of one. Why windows?

The final turn of the screw in the death of Elizabeth is Victor's sight of the Monster looking through the window glass (the wooden casement having been opened), grinning at her disrobed body and her husband enjoying his long-awaited moment of physical intimacy.

German has a word for a 'peeping Tom': *Spanner*. It is more forceful that the French *voyeur*. It carries the secondary meaning 'stretch' – as in standing on tiptoe the better to see what one shouldn't. The eight-foot Creature is not obliged to stretch to peek.

Grinning through the window, or from behind a curtain, by moonlight, is his modus operandi, as police detectives call the criminal's habitual practice. The first such incident is shortly after his birth, when Victor – always prone to fainting collapse – is lying flat out, fully dressed, on his four-poster bed, writhing in nightmare:

> I started from my sleep with horror; a cold dew covered my forehead, my teeth chattered, and every limb became convulsed; when, *by the dim and yellow light*

of the moon, as it forced its way through the window shutters, I beheld the wretch – the miserable monster whom I had created. He held up the curtain of the bed; and his eyes, if eyes they may be called, were fixed on me. His jaws opened, and he muttered some inarticulate sounds, *while a grin* wrinkled his cheeks. He might have spoken, but I did not hear; one hand was stretched out, seemingly to detain me, but I escaped and rushed downstairs. I took refuge in the courtyard belonging to the house which I inhabited, where I remained during the rest of the night, walking up and down in the greatest agitation, listening attentively, catching and fearing each sound as if it were to announce the approach of the demoniacal corpse to which I had so miserably given life. [my emphasis]

The second such scene is while Victor is creating his female monster:

I trembled and my heart failed within me, when, on looking up, I saw *by the light of the moon* the dæmon at the casement. *A ghastly grin* wrinkled his lips as he gazed on me, where I sat fulfilling the task which he had allotted to me. Yes, he had followed me in my travels; he had loitered in forests, hid himself in caves, or taken refuge in wide and desert heaths; and he now came to mark my progress and claim the fulfilment of my promise. [my emphasis]

The third such scene is, as described above (pages 167–8), Victor Frankenstein and the Monster's *ménage a trois* wedding night:

> While I still hung over her in the agony of despair, I happened to look up. The windows of the room had before been darkened, and I felt a kind of panic on seeing *the pale yellow light of the moon* illuminate the chamber. The shutters had been thrown back, and with a sensation of horror not to be described, I saw at the *open window* a figure the most hideous and abhorred. *A grin was on the face of the monster; he seemed to jeer,* as with his fiendish finger he pointed towards the corpse of my wife. [my emphasis]

These formulaic repetitions – moon, grin, window (curtain, casement) – might suggest a poverty of narrative imagination. They shouldn't. Windows are powerful images for paradoxical separation. Glass obstructs the arm reaching through it but allows the eye to view.

Paul makes the point in Corinthians, in one of the New Testament's most pregnant sentences. Heaven is a place without windows.

> For now we see through a glass, darkly; but then face to face: now I know in part; but then shall I know even as also I am known.

The window image, one recalls, is meaningfully central in *Wuthering Heights*. Heathcliff and Catherine die looking out of windows for something that may or may not be there. Henry James makes spine-chilling use of grinning Quint outside the window in *The Turn of the Screw*.*

In *Frankenstein* the monster looks through glass darkly (always in the dark of night, that is). The pale yellow (never 'gold') moon illuminates his hideous features. What the image creates is an entity which is both inside (inside Victor even, if one pursues the doppelganger, Jekyll and Hyde interpretation) and outside – inhuman. It's a finely woven thread in Mary Shelley's composition of her narrative. She did not need Roland Barthes to explain to her the workings of the symbolic code.

---

* The literary theorist Roland Barthes observes the significance of the window in the 'symbolic code', in his analysis of Balzac's *Sarrasine*, in *S/Z* (1970).

Does the Creature
have a passport?

႙ᆶ

F rontiers were not as strictly regulated in the 1790s as they would become in the 19th century. But legitimating documentation was often required. In his pursuit of Frankenstein and Clerval across the face of Europe, how does the Creature cross frontiers without let or hindrance?

Frankenstein's Creature rates among the most travelled *lusus naturae* in fiction – up there with Puck and Chewbacca. Closer to home (or Villa Diodati) one can align the Creature with that favourite legendary figure of the Romantic movement, and Shelley in particular, the Wandering Jew – cursed to roam the world until the Second Coming for having mocked Jesus on his way to Calvary. The legendary outcast does not merely wander – he is reviled, hated, spurned and maltreated wherever he goes.

Shelley had introduced the Wandering Jew centrally into *Queen Mab*, the poem which brought him into fateful contact with the Godwins and set him two years later on his own wandering path through life.

The following is from one of Shelley's explanatory notes in *Queen Mab*:

> Ahasuerus the Jew crept forth from the dark cave of Mount Carmel. Near two thousand years have elapsed since he was first goaded by never-ending restlessness to rove the globe from pole to pole.

One may note 'pole to pole'. Surviving handwritten notes elsewhere suggest that in 1815 Shelley was planning to write a novel on the Wandering Jew. Mary may be thought to have got there first.

Percy and Byron were reviled in England for their sexual delinquencies and obliged to wander through Europe to Switzerland in 1816. Both of them would be wanderers all their short lives. Mary was dragged along in their train, disowned, in the immediate aftermath of her elopement, even by her father.

The nested narrative of *Frankenstein* contains, as its 'hard core', a straightforward 'cut to the chase' thriller plot. In the first half of the narrative the Creature, once he has educated himself, chases his creator with vengeful intent. In the second half the creator chases the Creature with exterminatory intent. The twin pursuits carry the narrative thousands of miles. This is, roughly, the itinerary.

Victor Frankenstein is born in Naples but is moved, in early childhood, with his family to Geneva. The reason for the move is never clearly explained. In his late teens, now a confirmed Genevese, his primary language French, he goes to far-off Ingolstadt in Bavaria (as noted elsewhere, the reason behind the choice of institution is not explained) to study for several years. There it is, while still a student, that he makes his Creature.

The newborn entity flees to find refuge deep in the Bavarian forest. Victor meanwhile returns with his friend, Clerval, who has arrived to save him from himself, to the family home in Geneva.

Clerval is a student of modern languages, who has travelled all over Europe (a cosmopolitan Mary may have thought of doing something with this fact, but eventually didn't). Once he has learned to read, and has read Victor's journal, which he fortuitously picked up in Victor's workshop of filthy creation, the Creature follows the young men 400 miles from Germany to Switzerland. How is not explained.

Once arrived, the Creature tries to recruit William, Victor's young brother, as his companion. When he is rejected and abused he strangles the child. His lifelong revenge on humanity has begun. More murders follow. Now regarding himself as an outcast, he takes up hermit refuge in the icy mountains of Chamonix, on the *mer glace*, in sight of Mont Blanc. He loves the cold. He is now in France. There have been, for him, three countries of brief residence in a year.

Victor resolves to remove himself from any chance of encountering the Creature he now regards as a fiend from hell. He proposes a grand tour with Clerval – leaving his fiancée Elizabeth in Geneva. The tour takes the young men through Italy, France (currently in violent Revolutionary upheaval, undescribed), England (currently at war with France) and, finally, Scotland.

Keeping abreast and sometimes ahead of them, the Creature issues his demand his maker make him a mate – as God did for Adam. If he does, the paired Creatures will emigrate to South America. Reluctantly, Victor assents. He leaves Clerval in Perth, and takes himself to the northernmost point of Scotland, the Orkney Isles, for the operation. The Creature pursues him. When Victor loses his nerve, and destroys the female creature he has made, the foiled monster sails a small boat to Perth, abducts Clerval, then sails round the north of Scotland to Ireland, where he deposits his corpse.

Victor falls asleep in the drifting boat he has used to drop the remains of the female creature in the North Sea. He wakes to find himself in Ireland, exactly where the Creature disembarked. He, Victor, not the Creature, is apprehended for the murder of Clerval. There are, it seems, some very strange planetary magnetisms at work to create this fantastic coincidence. Mary Shelley, as usual, leaves it to us to work them out.

Victor is cleared of the murder and his father arrives to transport him back to Geneva, where he will belatedly marry Elizabeth – his 'sister' no more, but rather his future wife. On their wedding night at Evian the Monster, who has arrived before him, murders Elizabeth. Among other crimes, possibly.

Victor now sets out to destroy his Creature who, always faster, leads him on a chase through Turkey, Greenland and Russia to the Arctic regions.

Victor has been tracked over thousands of miles by the Creature, before himself turning pursuer. How? Was there some bloodhound in the slaughterhouses where Victor purloined animal body parts. Or is there is some ESP, which would account for the Monster's uncanny foreknowledge of where his maker is going? Victor, one deduces, can no more escape the Creature than Jekyll can escape Hyde. They are 'in' each other, 'of' each other. This it is which makes the two of them doppelgangers – literally 'double goers'. There is a lot of going in the novel.

The global toing and froing raises speculation. Frankenstein and Clerval, gentlemen with contacts in high places, will have some form of passports – of the late 18th-century kind, signed by some senior Genevese official. The Creature clearly would not qualify for documentation. But how does he cross all these frontiers without let or hindrance or even inconvenience? He can't use conventional transport – he has no money, and would be an unwelcome passenger. No one would want to share a stagecoach with an eight-foot 'mass of filth'. And homicidal to boot. The narrative is vague about his travels; as Victor says: 'he had followed me in my travels; he had loitered in forests, hid himself in caves, or taken refuge in wide and desert heaths'. But how does he cross the English Channel? It bears repeating: Britain is at war with France.

Why would authorities, even the local Dogberrys, not apprehend the Creature, wherever he rests. Does he, then, follow Victor on foot, smuggling himself across the Alps, swimming rivers and seas to keep up with his prey? His super-humanly intelligent mind gives him command, we apprehend, of at least three languages (French, German and English). But how does he make himself understood in Russia? If he did have a passport, what would his 'nationality' be?

Such questions swarm in on the puzzled reader of *Frankenstein*. Why does Mary Shelley make no effort to answer them? Because mystery, in this novel, works more powerfully than factual information and, one would like to think, is a deliberate impressionistic effect aimed at by her – like fog in a Pissarro painting.

The device (keep the reader grasping at straws) works in the novel but less well in film adaptation where the narrative holes and improbabilities yawn. Branagh's quixotically literalist film (a fascinatingly failed experiment in film adaptation) makes that clear. Spell it out, and you spoil the effect.

Why go to the North Pole
to commit suicide?

༄༅

The novel circles round to end where it began, in the Arctic. Why do the principals go north to finish things, and what does 'finish' mean?

Stage, screen, operatic and comic-book adaptations of *Frankenstein* conventionally wind the story up with the destruction of the Creature and his maker. Peake, in the 1823 play *Presumption* – a template for following adaptation – has the Creature shot by Victor, then both of them buried in an avalanche. Even in death they are not divided. Clerval (alive), Felix (who unconsciously taught the Creature to read), and the tinker Hammerpan (don't ask) observe the cataclysm breathlessly:

> **CLER.** Behold our friend and his mysterious enemy.
> **FELIX.** See – Frankenstein aims his musket at him – let us follow and assist him. *(Is going up stage with Clerval.)*
> **HAM.** Hold master! if the gun is fired, it will bring down a mountain of snow [on their heads.] Many an avalanche has fallen there.

[**FELIX.** He fires –]

*Music. – Frankenstein discharges his musket. – The
Demon and Frankenstein meet at the very extremity of
the stage. – Frankenstein fires – the avalanche falls and
annihilates the Demon and Frankenstein. – A heavy fall
of snow succeeds. – Loud thunder heard, and all the characters form a picture as the curtain falls.*

It strained the limited stage effects of 1823 but Peake pulled
it off. In the first surviving Thomas Edison film, of 1910,
the Creature rushes into a mirror and becomes – who else?
– Victor Frankenstein. This neat ending was clearly inspired
by the corpse of Mr Hyde morphing into the corpse of
Dr Jekyll in Stevenson's novel, itself a perennial favourite with
film-makers.

The most tremendous screen destruction of Frankenstein
was devised by James Whale. The Creature and creator, hounded by a lynch mob, expire together in a burning
windmill.

All these scenarios are knowingly unfaithful to what Mary
Shelley depicted. After Victor has quietly expired in his private cabin on Robert Walton's vessel the Creature, having paid
his obsequies to his maker, tells the captain what is next for
unhappy him:

Fear not that I shall be the instrument of future mischief. My work is nearly complete. Neither yours nor
any man's death is needed to consummate the series

of my being and accomplish that which must be done, but it requires my own. Do not think that I shall be slow to perform this sacrifice. I shall quit your vessel on the ice raft which brought me thither and shall seek the most northern extremity of the globe; I shall collect my funeral pile and consume to ashes this miserable frame, that its remains may afford no light to any curious and unhallowed wretch who would create such another as I have been. I shall die. I shall no longer feel the agonies which now consume me or be the prey of feelings unsatisfied, yet unquenched. He is dead who called me into being; and when I shall be no more, the very remembrance of us both will speedily vanish. I shall no longer see the sun or stars or feel the winds play on my cheeks. Light, feeling, and sense will pass away; and in this condition must I find my happiness. Some years ago, when the images which this world affords first opened upon me, when I felt the cheering warmth of summer and heard the rustling of the leaves and the warbling of the birds, and these were all to me, I should have wept to die; now it is my only consolation. Polluted by crimes and torn by the bitterest remorse, where can I find rest but in death?

'Farewell! I leave you ...'

Why is the Creature intending to cremate himself in 'the most northern extremity of the globe', rather than simply hurling himself into the icy waters? Or shooting himself with one of the pistols he is carrying? Or incinerating himself on some nearby iceberg, with some help from the crew who, one imagines, would not be averse to sending the Monster on his way?

One reason is suggested by the fate of Charles Byrne.* The Creature's body would be eagerly sought by science – especially in combination with Victor's working notes which, one presumes, he still carries with him. Walton could make a fortune out of him. By fire the Creature, and any putative progeny, will be irrecoverably exterminated – and by his own hand. A Roman death. Or suttee if, as we may suspect, he, at this last moment of their lives, has come, at last, to love his Creator – his 'father', as he elsewhere calls him.

But why the North Pole? It is, of course, where his ashes will never be found. No mere human has ever made it there, nor, Mary Shelley might have thought, ever would.

There is another reason. The North Pole is the geographical crossroads of the earth, where the cardinal directions north, south, east, and west meet and fuse magnetically into a point. The Creature's mortuary site is chosen for that reason and it relates to one of the crueller laws of Mary Shelley's time.

Suicide was defined as felo de se ('se offendendo', as the semi-literate gravedigger mangles the phrase, preparing a grave for suicidal Ophelia in *Hamlet*). It was 'self murder'. A crime against God. The Almighty, says Hamlet, has set his 'canon' against it.

---

* See above, pages 75–6.

So did England. It was decreed, by law, that the suicide's body should be buried at a crossroads, unceremoniously, with a stake through the heart. All the suicide's property might be forfeit. Crossroad burials of the suicide have been traced back to the Anglo-Saxon period. The requirement was revoked in 1823, as Mary Shelley was moving to her second edition. One reason was the sensational suicide of Lord Castlereagh in 1822 – the idea of burying a lord at the crossroads, with the conventional indignities, was unthinkable.

In practice, the fate was sometimes escapable, especially for members of nobility and gentry like Castlereagh. Percy's first wife Harriet and Mary's half-sister Fanny were also among those who committed suicide but avoided the barbarous crossroads punishment. Disgust at the law was brought to a head in London in 1823 with the case of Abel Griffiths who had killed himself and his father. A working-class man, the final indignity was visited on his body where the Victoria bus station now is.

The Creature wants a grand Wertherian death, inflamed as he has been by Goethe's romantic tale. It is the 1790s. He has chosen his own crossroads – roads that no mere human will ever cross.

Does the Creature
murder his 'father'?

༝༙༚

The climactic scenes of the novel take place in the ship's cabin where Victor dies and the Creature declares his resolution to die as well. Walton is talked out of killing the Creature. Details are scarce.

'The Being' (as Walton calls him) claims to have killed Victor. There is an artful unclarity in the claim. Earlier in the novel, for example, Victor calls himself the murderer of little William by having loosed into the world the monster who killed him. He also calls himself the murderer of Justine, framed for a crime which she did not commit, whom Victor could have saved by confessing all. He was not strictly their murderer but party to their deaths. The Creature murders William, Clerval, Elizabeth and an unidentified fisherman. But does he, in the full sense of the word, murder Victor?

When last seen, Victor is at death's door. His last words are to his new friend, Walton, who has comforted his dying days. Victor's warmest, most physical friendships are always with his own sex. Beds figure, as here on Walton's vessel and in Ingolstadt, where Clerval nursed him back to health.

But face it Victor must in his last moments: his mission – to kill the Creature he made and save humanity – is now forlorn. He could not kill a flea, let alone a superman.

'My judgment and ideas,' Victor tells Walton, 'are already disturbed by the near approach of death.' But he almost asks Walton to do what he, Victor, cannot do: kill the beast:

> I dare not ask you to do what I think right, for I may still be misled by passion. That he should live to be an instrument of mischief disturbs me; in other respects, this hour, when I momentarily expect my release, is the only happy one which I have enjoyed for several years. The forms of the beloved dead flit before me, and I hasten to their arms. Farewell, Walton!* Seek happiness in tranquility and avoid ambition.

With this banal advice on his lips Victor expires. His dangerous knowledge goes with him.

> His voice became fainter as he spoke, and at length, exhausted by his effort, he sank into silence. About half an hour afterwards he attempted again to speak but was unable; he pressed my hand feebly, and his eyes closed for ever, while the irradiation of a gentle smile passed away from his lips.

---

* He too echoes Werther (see page 140).

Walton's next action is very odd. He does not call the ship's surgeon (there is one on board). He does not stay a minute with the man whom fortune threw his way to be his best friend. What does Walton do? He goes at once to his cabin, to update his sister on what has been going on, and forewarn her to expect his return as fast as fair wind and canvas can carry him.

Since the nearest postal service is in Archangel, and delivery from there will be slower than a ship under sail, it seems strange – unless we assume the obsessive letter writing is neurotic, like the obsessive-compulsive's handwashing. Or, perhaps, Walton fears that any voyage home may be impossible. His vessel will be smashed to splinters by floes, or crushed by pack ice. His letters to Margaret are his last testament to whomever finds him.

For the last possible time in the novel we wonder who is the 'Saville' whose surname his sister Margaret bears. We shall never know. And we shall never know more about Walton's background than we know about that of the ancient mariner or Melville's Ishmael.

And what, one wonders, is Captain Walton going to do with Victor Frankenstein's body? Cast it with the conventional obsequies into the waves? Preserve it in ice (plenty of that around) till they strike land (if they ever do) and send it on to Geneva so that, in the last day, he shall rise with his mother, the only woman Victor has ever loved? Dunk the mortal remains of the heroic scientist in a barrel of brandy, as was done to Nelson's body after Trafalgar? Such details niggle.

There may be a hinted answer a little later when Walton refers to the newly dead Victor lying in his 'coffin' (i.e. bunk). This could be taken to suggest burial at sea. Bodies were consigned into the ocean wrapped in canvas, routinely taken from their bedding. A historical precursor of the modern body bag.

It is now the witching hour – midnight. Still writing the catch-up letter to Margaret, while Victor's mortal remains are cooling a few feet away, Walton hears something. Has Victor come back to life? The narrative breaks into present tense with the excitement of the moment (a routine device with epistolary narrators like Samuel Richardson):

> I am interrupted. What do these sounds portend? It
> is midnight; the breeze blows fairly, and the watch
> on deck scarcely stir. Again there is a sound as of a
> human voice, but hoarser; it comes from the cabin
> where the remains of Frankenstein still lie.

'Still' lie? How could the remains be anywhere else? Or does Walton mean 'stilly lie'?

When he rushes into the neighbouring cabin, Walton encounters a blood-chilling sight. The massive 'Being' has, with his monstrous agility, directed an ice raft towards Walton's vessel and coupled with it. How he can have done so is a mystery. One may linger a moment to describe what this 'raft' is – it will figure again, climactically, and should not be confused with, say, the raft which is central in *Huckleberry Finn*. It is a thin floe of ice, not an amphibious version of the wooden sled which the Creature is described by Walton as using earlier. An ice raft is not navigable. It drifts whither tide and wave arbitrarily take it.

The vessel must, even in these remote waters and with a mutinous crew, have set watches: men on guard. That they would not notice a giant, without side-rigging, clamber aboard speaks ill of the discipline under Walton's command. But how did the Monster direct his 'raft' to get close enough to board the ship? More curiously, how did the Monster know, precisely and to the very hour, that his Creator (or alter ego?) was *in articulo mortis* – at the point of death? It is not the only occasion in the novel that he seems endowed with ESP.

Back to Walton, pen in hand, ear cocked. 'I must arise and examine,' he writes. 'Good night, my sister.' The full stop indicates what will be a pause of some hours. Then (back to the past tense) Walton returns to continue the letter:

Great God! what a scene has just taken place! I am yet dizzy with the remembrance of it. I hardly know whether I shall have the power to detail it; yet the tale which I have recorded would be incomplete without this final and wonderful catastrophe.

I entered the cabin where lay the remains of my ill-fated and admirable friend. Over him hung a form which I cannot find words to describe – gigantic in stature, yet uncouth and distorted in its proportions. As he hung over the coffin, his face was concealed by long locks of ragged hair; but one vast hand was

extended, in colour and apparent texture like that of
a mummy. When he heard the sound of my approach,
he ceased to utter exclamations of grief and horror
and sprung towards the window. Never did I behold
a vision so horrible as his face, of such loathsome yet
appalling hideousness. I shut my eyes involuntarily
and endeavoured to recollect what were my duties
with regard to this destroyer. I called on him to stay.

Somewhat reckless, one might think, given the entity's habitual way with Victor's best friends.

Mary Shelley, as is now clear, did not know much about
seagoing ships. Polar-voyaging vessels did not have windows
for icebergs to break and certainly no fenestration large
enough for an eight-foot ('gigantic in stature') creature to
find unimpeded ingress and egress. Or 'spring through' as he
later does, glass being no impediment to either his coming or
going. How, incidentally, did the Creature know in which cabin
Victor was lying and dying? He has never been within miles
of Walton's vessel.

Walton continues, eager to tell his sister, 5,000 miles
away, what happens next:

He paused, looking on me with wonder, and again
turning towards the lifeless form of his creator, he
seemed to forget my presence, and every feature and
gesture seemed instigated by the wildest rage of some
uncontrollable passion.

'That is also my victim!' he exclaimed. 'In his murder my crimes are consummated; the miserable series of my being is wound to its close! Oh, Frankenstein! Generous and self-devoted being! What does it avail that I now ask thee to pardon me? I, who irretrievably destroyed thee by destroying all thou lovedst. Alas! He is cold, he cannot answer me.'

In what way, since he here confesses the act, can the Creature be thought to have murdered Victor? Most plausibly by cat-and-mousing the poor man to die in a place where he would experience for himself the same existential loneliness which has tortured the Creature. Walton's sailing in, out of the blue, frustrated the last twist of the knife.

And what, in the final analysis, is the relationship between Frankenstein and what he has engendered? One recalls the Creature's remark, on reading Victor's scientific log: 'I learned from your papers that you were my father, my creator'. Now he is Victor's Oedipus.

So what now for the Creature, now that his great game is over? 'I shall quit your vessel on the ice raft which brought me thither,' he tells Walton,

and shall see the most northern extremity of the globe; I shall collect my funeral pile and consume to ashes this miserable frame, that its remains may afford no light to any curious and unhallowed wretch who would create such another as I have been. I shall die.

> He sprang from the cabin-window as he said this,
> upon the ice raft which lay close to the vessel. He was
> soon borne away by the waves and lost in darkness
> and distance.

Mary Shelley has temporarily forgotten there is no darkness in the polar region, the land of the midnight sun, in summer. It is September. The sun still shines 24 hours a day.

Luckily, but not entirely plausibly, the untethered ice raft is still precisely under the improbably large 'window', twenty-odd feet below. An hour before, the waves bore the Creature towards Walton's ship. Now the same waves bear him away from it. How? Kinetic energy? An unmentioned paddle? Does he have microclimatic powers and can raise a favourable wind? And how, without locomotive power (his dogs must surely after all these months have starved) will he get himself to the north-ernmost point of the pole to incinerate himself into ash.

A last puzzle: what exactly is the Creature going to use as fuel for his proposed 'pyre'? His sled, wherever it is, and Victor's notes will supply kindling but there is nothing combustible at the North Pole. You cannot burn snow. If anything, the ice will preserve the Creature as in very frigid places on earth it has preserved the woolly mammoth.

It all raises a final speculation. Will Walton's vessel ever be able to leave? If it remains immovably locked in pack ice its timber could furnish a fine bonfire when the crew and the armed Walton die of starvation on board. Or he might lose patience and kill them. The Creature could then perish in the flames with the body of Victor Frankenstein, the man he now loves.

In the vacancies Mary Shelley left one is driven to invent unwritten narratives. Other more inventive readers than I (possibly a writer or two) will create alternatives to match the best endings of the best films. Myself, I plump for Whale's burning windmill as the best of many conclusions currently in stock.

III.
AFTERTHOUGHTS

Frankenstein in film

∂⌐

Undoubtedly, the most imaginative Frankenstein films supplement Mary Shelley's novel creatively. And it could be argued that in certain key ways they add to what we find on her page.

Which, though, are those best films? James Whale's 1931 modern-dress classic has been frequently referred to as such; a string of Hammer gothics directed by Terence Fisher starring Peter Cushing, from 1957 onwards, are first rate; Mel Brooks's 1974 burlesque *Young Frankenstein* and Kenneth Branagh's 1994 blockbuster *Mary Shelley's Frankenstein* explore aspects of the novel creatively.

A lower level of films manifestly travesty their source. But even the most extreme of them can have interest. My favourite B-movie 'knock-off', *Frankenhooker*, for example, features exploding prostitutes. Pity the last client.

One can even extract a useful laugh from *Frankenstein: the College Years* (being eight feet tall helps no end on the basketball court). *The Rocky Horror Picture Show* has become an institutional burlesque in the US with its Dr Frank N. Furter and his creation Rocky. When we lived in Pasadena (home of *Teen Wolf*) my young son went religiously to a Saturday-night showing at the Rialto cinema (famous from Robert Altman's

The Player) in gothic fig, where a similarly clad audience of like age would indulge in a popcorn fight and chant their favourite lines along with the film. Thirty years later, my son, alas, has yet to read *Frankenstein*.

What superior film versions do, given their necessarily tight narrative space, is strip off the novel's three-volume surplus. Films routinely remove Shelley's Arctic frame (Kenneth Branagh is an exception). Similarly cut away is the double flashback strand via Victor's and the Creature's narratives. The Creature's woodland pedagogy rarely gets space. Promethean, Miltonic, and Aeschylean reference is dropped for mass audiences. Contemporary (i.e. 1818 contemporary) scientific reference is typically replaced with plausibly modern mumbo-jumbo.

Also blanked out are some of the grosser improbabilities. For example, Victor assembling his creature single-handed, unnoticed, in a cramped undergraduate's study, where there are more books than apparatus. The films fabricate, for plausibility's sake, a proper laboratory setting for the operation which brings the creature to life. And most of the best films, as I think them, rationalise Mary's 1790s 'hideous idea' by transposing it to a later period, where genuinely modern biological science can come into play. Erasmus Darwin, cited in the first line of the 1818 book, is nowhere in any film I've seen (or can remember).

One recalls that the novel began as an oral performance, at Villa Diodati, in June 1816. Before the moving film arrived, in the early 20th century, *Frankenstein* had established itself as a popular melodrama and burlesque and had seeped from the stage into proverbial and folkloric currency. It was commonplace for Victorian cartoonists to denigrate rampaging working-class or Irish mobs as 'Frankensteins'. There were, as Steven Forry calculates, over ninety different dramatisations of Mary Shelley's novel in the 19th century – almost as many as there were films in the 20th.*

As has been discussed elsewhere, the earliest trend-setting, long-running theatre adaptation was *Presumption; Or, the Fate of Frankenstein*, by Richard Brinsley Peake, five years after the novel's first publication. Mary saw it in the company of her (by then reconciled) father. She particularly liked the way the actor playing the Creature, Thomas Cooke, tried to grasp sounds with his hands. Cooke had, two years before, played the ghoul in a stage adaptation of Polidori's *The Vampyre*.

Mary may well have thought Peake's invention of the clownish assistant, Fritz, useful. But there were aspects of the adaptation she could not have entirely liked. Peake had moralised her story, as the judgemental title 'Presumption' declares.†

Peake did not show the presumptuous creation of the Creature on stage. A 'sudden combustion' is viewed through a peephole by the on-stage Fritz – whose flabbergasted response was designed to provoke laughter alongside the thrills. On

....

* http://knarf.english.upenn.edu/Articles/forry2.html

† For the full text of *Presumption* see: https://frankensteinscreature.wordpress .com/presumption-or-the-fate-of-frankenstein-1823-play/

stage, the lighting flickered from blue to red. From off-stage rings out Victor's exclamation (picked up a century later by any number of film makers): 'It Lives! It Lives!'

Fritz's response? 'Oh, dear!' The poor fellow shakes like a leaf at the sight, through his peephole, of a 'hob goblin, seven and twenty feet high'. And blue skinned. The audience is in suspense – will a giant that size really appear on stage? Victor, after examining what it is that 'lives' rushes out, in disgust. He has seen, he says, the 'dull yellow eye'. It's enough.

The subsequent 19th-century theatrical versions, lacking a complex stage machinery with which to simulate 'creation' or gigantism (though Cooke was an unusually tall actor), presented, as had Peake, a monster manufactured by alchemy or some *elixir vitae*. And considerably short of 27 feet.

What the best films would do, when their technology came in at the end of the century, was to focus attention on a paramount issue in the novel. Is the creation of life a male or female act? The issue can be summarised as: the bath (womb) or the bolt (phallus).

The first serious film version of *Frankenstein* was produced by Thomas A. Edison's company, in 1910.* Although Edison was the Messiah of electricity, this primal *Frankenstein* had the creature hatched, and grown from seed, in a bathtub, full of a warm (clearly amniotic) fluid. The monster is delivered, steamily, from a metallic womb.

....

* Happily the film survives and has been remastered. It is available, currently, on YouTube.

Although the film is primitive, with one fixed camera, one set, and only thirteen minutes running time, it has subtle turns of plot. The monster invades Victor's home and is confronted by a full-length mirror. It enters the mirror. When Victor looks, he sees himself reflected and disappears into the infinite. It's an imaginative conclusion.

Ask most people what brings the Creature to life and the answer will not be a warm uterine bath but lightning. It was, in point of fact, a 1915 Broadway stage adaptation, called *The Last Laugh*, which picked up on Mary Shelley's 1831 afterthought about galvanism by introducing electrical machinery into the creation scene. For most films, lightning is the so-called 'money shot'.

For the 1931 Universal Pictures production, its massive laboratory set was dominated by huge electro-galvanic generators, designed by Kenneth Strickfaden, and inspired by Nikola Tesla's dramatic electricity shows.* But James Whale, the *auteur* director, was more directly influenced by an elaborately staged scene in Fritz Lang's dystopian epic *Metropolis* (1926), where a robot is electrically activated. Whale carried over into his lumbering Karloff-creation of Frankenstein's 'monster' a robotic clumsiness and total inarticulacy – not to mention two electro-metallic terminals sticking out from his head. It is wholly contrary to Shelley's highly literate, superhumanly

....

* See the Smithsonian account of Tesla's life, works, and long feud with Edison: https://www.smithsonianmag.com/innovation/extraordinary-life -nikola-tesla-180967758/

intelligent and athletically lithe monster, who trains himself in human emotion by reading Goethe's *Sorrows of Young Werther*, is an expert rock-climber and can swim faster than a seal. On a diet of berries.

The point, however, is that the lightning bolt is phallic. It is the firmament's ejaculation of seed. James Whale's *Frankenstein* has no foreground female characters. Neither has Mary Shelley's novel, it could be argued. Whale filled the gender gap with *Bride of Frankenstein*. Shelley never did – although having left the Creature alive at the end of the narrative, she could have done.

The main filmic distortion of Shelley's original conception of Victor Frankenstein can be laid at the door of the novelist herself. Writing in her 1831 preface the author muses about how the great experiment *might* have been achieved:

> Perhaps a corpse would be reanimated; galvanism had given token of such things: perhaps the component parts of a creature might be manufactured, brought together, and endued with vital warmth.

Shelley enlarges on this idea, picturing some

> pale student of unhallowed arts kneeling beside the thing he had put together. I saw the hideous phantasm of a man stretched out, and then, on the working of some powerful engine, show signs of life, and stir with an uneasy, half-vital motion.

Most films have taken up Shelley's afterthought hint. The electro-robotic Karloffian stereotype dominated popular reproductions for decades after. By the 1990s, however, bio-genetics had taken over from electro-physics as the cutting-edge science in the popular imagination. What relativity was in the 1920s, when Whale created his film, the Human Genome Project now was. As Kenneth Branagh notes in his afterword to the 'novelization' of *Mary Shelley's Frankenstein*:

> We hope audiences [of the 1994 film] today may find parallels with Victor today in some amazing scientist who might be an inch away from curing AIDS or cancer and needs to make some difficult decisions.

This was a new turn in the *Frankenstein* industry, and reflected the state of things at the end of the 20th century.

What Branagh's film shared with its predecessors, however, is a morbid fascination with the scientific details of the creation process. In the film's novelization text three chapters are expended on mechanical description of the great experiment. We are taken painstakingly through the manufacture of the gigantic copper sarcophagus (i.e. womb) in which the embryonic monster is suspended, the collection of body parts (including the *de rigueur* genius's brain), the pooling of many buckets of amniotic fluid into a sufficient placenta, and the construction of the electrical generating apparatus (with a tankful of electric eels as back-up – a finely surreal touch).

Mary Shelley's source narrative is intrinsically different from film treatments – even Branagh's, which loyally proclaims itself *Mary Shelley's* and does its quixotic best to be faithful to her.

One of the remarkable things about Mary Shelley's novel is that it remakes itself, and reframes adaptations, with every scientific parameter shift: from Creationism to Darwinism to Einsteinian physics to robotics, AI and DNA.

There will, it is a certainty, be more spirit-of-the-(scientific)-age *Frankensteins* to come. It is a novel for all seasons.

Chips off the Frankenstein block

༊༔

F*rankenstein* has a long history of offshoots on stage, screen and page. It has become part of our lives, folkloric – no need to read the book.

Danny Boyle's 2012 National Theatre production, starring Benedict Cumberbatch, is remembered as epochal: the millennial adaptation. More recently, in 2018, there was a teacup storm in *The Times* about whether the Creature should be considered a #MeToo-style abuse victim. There is a learned 2017 monograph about the novel and the rights of children.* And much more. Signs of life, one could call them. Signs of immortality even.

On the web are found such wares as the 'Frankenstein Munster Tampon Case' which, as its merchandiser boasts, 'protects tampons from getting wet or crushed in your purse, and also protects credit cards from RFID theft and demagnetization. Image is protected with a strong UV-resistant coating.' This means, I think, that it will not decay in sunlight, like Dracula.

....
* Eileen Hunt Botting, *Mary Shelley and the Rights of the Child: Political Philosophy in* Frankenstein (2017)

'Munster' alludes to the 1960s TV series *The Munsters*, chronicling a happy Frankensteinian Californian family, in the Eisenhower good years, presided over by the Karloff lookalike patriarch Herman.

More interesting, because more cynical, was the rival show, *The Addams Family*. Originating in Charles Adams's supremely ironic *New Yorker* cartoons, it was developed into a sixties TV series, films, and various running adaptations all making the point that you shouldn't take the American middle-class family as what the soap advertisements claim it to be. The Addamses' needs are catered to by the Karloffian manservant Lurch (a jest on the monster's high heels in James Whale's film, which meant the star could never walk straight). One likes to think Mary Shelley would have found *The Addams Family* easy viewing.

The prefix 'Franken-' is ubiquitous. The latest I've come across is 'Frankenproduct' – computers which slash the price of the store-bought commodity by assembling an array of parts from different sources (not, one hastens to say, dug up with shovel and sack from the landfill).

Frankenstein porn knock-offs (as they're called) are an industry. *F*ckenstein* (my asterisk) may be too broad, even for the broad-minded. The cultural interest is the way in which porn knock-offs masculinise a novel which is, canonically, a feminine and feminist work by the daughter of the most venerated feminist in British history.

Great writers have found inspirations, small and large, in *Frankenstein*. By the mid-19th century the word had become common shorthand allusion. In her social problem novel, *Mary Barton*, Mrs Gaskell breaks off from depicting the suffering of her opium-ruined, murderous mill worker John Barton to declare, in authorial hushed voice:

> But what availed his sympathy? No education had given him wisdom; and without wisdom, even love, with all its effects, too often works but harm. He acted to the best of his judgement, but it was a widely erring judgement.
>
> The actions of the uneducated seem to me typified in those of Frankenstein, that monster of many human qualities, ungifted with a soul, a knowledge of the difference between good and evil.
>
> The people rise up to life; they irritate us, they terrify us, and we become their enemies. Then, in the sorrowful moment of our triumphant power, their eyes gaze on us with mute reproach. Why have we made them what they are; a powerful monster, yet without the inner means for peace and happiness?
>
> John Barton became a Chartist, a Communist ...

And, the novel goes on to show us, a murderer.

Gaskell was writing *Mary Barton* in 1847, a year before the *Communist Manifesto* was published and the so-called year of revolutions. Marx and Engels had written their work in Manchester's Chetham Library, less than a mile from where the novelist (a Unitarian) was getting her novel into shape. A strange Mancunian collocation.

Gaskell makes the invariable mistake of calling the monster 'Frankenstein', but she understands perfectly what Mary Shelley, Godwin's daughter as well as Wollstonecraft's, was getting at: society makes essentially good people into monsters then destroys them – or they destroy their makers. Society makes crime, it does not suppress crime. There are links between Godwinism and intellectual Unitarianism.

Dickens is more constructive in his use of Mary Shelley. Boz's first literary purchases with his scant pocket money, as a little boy, had been tuppenny 'Tales of Terror'. 'Dreadfuls' as they were called; pulp versions of *Frankenstein* were a main ware.

In *Great Expectations* (Chapter 40), Pip observes, parenthetically, of his 'maker' Magwitch:

> The imaginary student pursued by the misshapen creature he had impiously made, was not more wretched than I, pursued by the creature who had made me, and recoiling from him with a stronger repulsion, the more he admired me and the fonder he was of me.

Dickens, describing the Creature's love-hate relationship with Victor, had evidently read the novel carefully.

Another echo is heard in *Middlemarch*, Chapter 15, and its description of Lydgate's great quest, the discovery of 'primary webs and tissues':

The more he became interested in special questions of disease, such as the nature of fever or fevers, the more keenly he felt the need for that fundamental knowledge of structure which just at the beginning of the century had been illuminated by the brief and glorious career of Bichat, who died when he was only one-and-thirty, but, like another Alexander, left a realm large enough for many heirs. That great Frenchman first carried out the conception that living bodies, fundamentally considered, are not associations of organs which can be understood by studying them first apart, and then as it were federally; but must be regarded as consisting of certain primary webs or tissues, out of which the various organs – brain, heart, lungs, and so on – are compacted, as the various accommodations of a house are built up in various proportions of wood, iron, stone, brick, zinc, and the rest, each material having its peculiar composition and proportions. No man, one sees, can understand and estimate the entire structure or its parts – what are its frailties and what its repairs, without knowing the nature of the materials.

George Eliot is not directly echoing *Frankenstein*; she is 'evolving' the novel's ideas, to use a term appropriate to her post-Darwinian period.

Stevenson's *Dr Jekyll and Mr Hyde* similarly evolves *Frankenstein*'s doppelganger theme ('the Creature is me'). So too Wilde's *Dorian Gray*. There is for Dorian no workshop of filthy creation but an attic, in which in the inner (real) Dorian decays into filth.

In my judgement, the Victorian novel which most creatively uses *Frankenstein* is that which stays closest to its main idea – that scientists can make man – H.G. Wells's *The Island of Dr Moreau* (1896). The central action takes place on a Pacific island where Dr Moreau, earlier hounded out of England for torturing animals, has perfected techniques of vivisection by which he can accelerate evolution.

Under Moreau's scalpel brutes are raised to quasi-humanity. Pain and moral severity are used to keep the animalic 'humans' in check lest their old instincts break out. Rebellion and bloodlust finally do erupt. The animal in man cannot be caged. Moreau is killed by a panther he was tormenting into biped humanity.

Worth citing is the Mary Shelley homage *The Purple Cloud*, by M.P. Shiel (1900). The hero voyages to the North Pole (which man had still not yet reached). Its polar centre is warm – Eden is regained. But meanwhile a toxic cloud has destroyed all mankind. The hero, like Shelley's Creature, is cosmically alone. The last of his kind.* 'Thanks to Mary Shelley' should be the epithet on this and many other works of Victorian Gothic and proto-science fiction.

In the 20th century Brian Aldiss's *Frankenstein Unbound* (1973) has peculiar interest. Aldiss sees Mary Shelley's novel

....

* See my Introduction to the Penguin Classics edition of *The Purple Cloud* (2012) for a discussion of Shiel's use of the Arktos myths also invoked by Shelley.

as science fiction's big bang, the literary moment when the genre came into being. Aldiss's allusion to *Prometheus Unbound* signals that Percy is in the mix somewhere.

Frankenstein Unbound was written in the icy depths of the Cold War and reflects that fact. Things have, in 2020, got very hot. A nuclear big bang slips Joe Bodenland back in time to the banks of Lake Geneva in 1816.

Fact and fiction melt into each other. Frankenstein, his Creature, its mate (it too 'lives'), Mary Shelley (love interest for Bodenland), Byron and Percy Shelley all exist on the same narrative plane. Time has dissolved, so has history. The novel's thesis is manifest. If you want to write science fiction, asserts Aldiss, you must make love to Mary Shelley. Not literally (although Bodenland comes close), but literarily.

Roger Corman, the preeminent practitioner of Gothic cinema, filmed *Frankenstein Unbound* (1990). Not everyone liked the result; but Corman's smart way with horror and fantasy was always experimental, and more influential with fellow directors than with audiences.* Nick Brimble's monster was generally applauded among Corman cult admirers. Up there with Karloff, it was judged. Corman took the million dollars he was paid and smiled all the way to the bank. Posterity has come to value the film as an imaginative supplement to its two sources, Shelley and Aldiss.†

....

* Francis Ford Coppola, the director of *Bram Stoker's Dracula* (1992) and producer of *Mary Shelley's Frankenstein* (1994) was a Corman apprentice and disciple.

† The film, well worth viewing, is currently available on YouTube.

1973 was a good year for Frankenstein revivals. In addition to *Frankenstein Unbound* it also saw the underrated *Frankenstein: The True Story*. The primary reason for its being underrated is that makers could not decide which medium would best serve the story. It began as a TV miniseries. It was then compacted into a film. Then the writers, Christopher Isherwood (no less) and his partner, the artist Don Bachardy, irritated by what they saw as the mishandling of their ideas, finally published their script and screenplay, in 2012, which is the best place to start.

In the authors' original screenplay William, Victor's young brother, is drowned. Victor embarks on a crusade to eradicate death. He is aided by Clerval, now a scientist who has cracked the secret of reanimation. Clerval's heart fails as the creation process is near completion. His brain is transplanted into the Creature.

The Creature is beautiful. Victor enters into a love relationship with him – something he could not do with Clerval when living. There are period scenes in English high society where the Creature is universally admired. But physical rot sets in. The monster, unable to live with ugliness, tries and fails to kill himself. John Polidori is introduced, latterly, as a villainous reanimator – played, with his familiar sinister suavity, by James Mason. It climaxes with a polar ice-fall, recalling, distantly, *Presumption.**

....

* The TV version can currently be found on YouTube. See also http://www
.littleshoppeofhorrors.com/LSoH38.htm

Isherwood and Bachardy's 'true story' is the fullest exploration of the gay undertones of Mary Shelley's novel – something which she could only hint at subversively in 1818. *Frankenstein* had at last come out.

The most arresting recent exploitation of Shelley's infinitely rich novel is the prize-winning* bestseller *Frankenstein in Baghdad*, by Ahmed Saadawi. The story is post-traumatic. More people have been blown to bits in Iraq in the last twenty years than anywhere in the world since the Second World War. Baghdad is a city of unattached body parts.

Saadawi's novel is set two years after the Gulf War. One narrative focus is on a multiply bereaved Christian widow, Elishva. Saddam killed her son. The US have killed her town. They are now its 'occupiers'. She believes in resurrection and may, some of her neighbours think, have 'powers'.

One of those neighbours is Hadi, 'a junk dealer with bulging eyes, who reeked of alcohol'. He conducts his business from a shed in property abandoned by Jewish owners fleeing persecution. The 'Jewish ruin' it is called.

Hadi has seen the Kenneth Branagh–Robert De Niro *Frankenstein* and aims to collect and sort body parts so their owners can have a proper burial. Bodies, even parts of them, this commonest of common men believes, should not be treated as 'trash'.

Hadi runs to the scene of one of the explosions which rock Baghdad daily:

....
* It won the Arabic International Prize for Fiction in 2014.

The smell suddenly hit his nostrils – the smoke, the burning of plastic and seat cushions, the roasting of human flesh. You wouldn't have smelled anything like it in your life and would never forget it.

Hadi always has a canvas sack with him; he picks up a nose, 'still coated in congealed, dark red blood' from the smoking debris. Just what the junk dealer has been looking for. In his workshop he attaches it to a 'massive' but noseless corpse he has been storing. The nose fits. Hadi has now created a 'man of parts'. He is called 'Whatsitsname' – Mary Shelley would doubtless have approved, as she approved of Peake's '------'.

As does Mary Shelley's Creature, Whatsitsname, now possessed by a shattered security guard's soul, runs off to embark on a destructive rampage, avenging the shattered corpses of Baghdad. Elishva gives him shelter.

His acts make the newspapers, along with the never-ending post-war bombs. The alarmed authorities call on soothsayers and astrologers. And, of course, the military. Whatsitsname begins to fall apart. So does everything else. War will do that.

Frankenstein in Baghdad is, Anglophone critics found, not an easy novel to read – Arabic fiction does not follow the story-telling conventions of its Western counterpart. But Saadawi's novel proves, yet again, how Mary Shelley's founding idea adapts to whatever time and place it finds itself. And will do so forever, one expects.

Dracula versus Frankenstein
– who wins?

჻

Dracula vs. Frankenstein (1971) is, on the face of it, an abysmal film. Directed by Al Adamson, the essence of the movie's early seventies appeal is captured by the poster shout line: 'LOVE TRAMPS – seduced by CREATURES from the GRAVE!' It's on a par, one might assume, with *Abbott and Costello Meet Frankenstein*. To be honest, when I saw that burlesque aged ten, in 1948, I laughed fit to split my sides. I still love it.* And latterly I have come to believe it throws a valuable sidelight, as burlesque often can, on *Frankenstein*'s achievement. It is a novel always reaching out from itself, often to unexpected places.

Dracula vs. Frankenstein trades on the permissive attitude to porn movies at a period when that dubious genre's classics (*The Devil in Miss Jones, Behind the Green Door, Deep Throat, Cry Uncle*) were being made.† A point of interest is that one of the *Dracula vs. Frankenstein*'s consultants, and actors, was Forrest

....

* So does the US Library of Congress, which deems the Bud and Lou comic romp 'culturally significant' and has placed it in the National Film Registry. Clips are available on YouTube.

† See Kenneth Turan, *Sinema* (1974).

J. Ackerman, the great connoisseur and collector of all things gothic, horror, and science fiction. Stephen King, a friend in later life, described him as the 'World's Greatest Science Fiction Fan'. At age eleven King had actually submitted a story to Ackerman, in his literary agent capacity. Politely rejected, apparently. Steven Spielberg and George Lucas were other admirers.

Ackerman was the editor of the fanzine *Famous Monsters of Filmland* – Frankenstein's monster being among the most famous. A cult hero, based in Los Angeles, Ackerman went on to play bit parts in such grimy B-movie classics as *Braindead* (1992) and *Nudist Colony of the Dead* (1991). As a literary agent he represented, among other luminaries, Ray Bradbury and L. Ron Hubbard before the founder of scientology discovered more profitable markets for fantasy than science fiction. More to the point here, Ackerman wrote, among much else with distant connections to the Villa Diodati, *The Frankenscience Monster*.

Ackerman merits attention as representative of the seething cultural depths in which *Frankenstein* has afterlife. One cannot register the full range of what Mary Shelley left the world unless one at least casts a glance at works like *Dracula vs. Frankenstein*. Or, come to that, *Abbott and Costello Meet Frankenstein*. *F*ckenstein* can be avoided.

Adamson's film was released and re-released under a welter of alternative titles: *Blood of Frankenstein* (in the UK), *The Revenge of Dracula*, *Teenage Dracula* and *They're Coming to Get You*. It's currently, as I write (I've just spent a merry hour and 33 minutes re-watching it), available on YouTube. It follows the attempts of a wheelchair-bound mad scientist,

Dr Durea (recalling Dr Strangelove), the last descendant of Victor Frankenstein, and his mute assistant Groton (played by horror veteran Lon Chaney Jr) – quite as inept as Whale's Fritz – to resurrect the body of the Creature. Durea is assisted by Dracula, himself hoping for the reward of a serum which will make him immune to sunlight.

Dracula vs. Frankenstein reminds us that these two immensely inspirational icons were 'created', to use the appropriate word, in an atmosphere of sportive winner-takes-all competition. The Shelleys took the literary field, pens raised, versus Byron, Clairmont and Polidori. Mary and Polidori were the last two standing. But who won – still wins – the Villa Diodati game? The vampire or the Creature?

Polidori's *The Vampyre* took off into popular fame faster than *Frankenstein*, as a result of Henry Colburn's unscrupulously publishing it not as an interesting exploration of Byronism – which it is – but as a work by Byron himself.*

It was then piratically dramatised as *The Vampire* (formally known as *The Vampire; Or, The Bride of the Isles*) by James Robinson Planché, in 1820 at the Lyceum Theatre, London, with Thomas Cooke in the lead. Cooke would play Frankenstein's monster at the English Opera House three years later.

The immensely popular, much reprinted penny serial for the masses, *Varney the Vampire; Or, the Feast of Blood* (1847) by James Rymer, and multiple other like works gave Polidori's invention the edge over the course of the 19th century. In the

....
* For Colburn's misbehaviour and Byron's indignant response see John Sutherland and Veronica Melnyk, *Rogue Publisher: Henry Colburn* (2018).

1890s when the late Byronic cult of ennui, style and deca-
dence was at its height, *Dracula* (1897) by Bram Stoker put
dark wings on Polidori's sketch. *Frankenstein*, by contrast, was
lumbering.

Vampirism, as an exploitable theme, had more political
potential for adaptors catering to mass audiences. The ghoul in
a dress coat could be played as a predatory aristocrat – something hallmarked by Bela Lugosi. The vampiric 'monster'
needed fewer special effects, other than overdeveloped canines,
a foreign accent, and a naked female neck.

What gave *Dracula* the advantage over *Frankenstein* was
its sexual potential. Ruthven in Polidori's foundational story
is closely based on Byron: poet and predator. In his diary, the
young physician recounts their arrival at an inn on the way to
the Villa Diodati: 'As soon as he reached his room, Lord Byron
fell like a thunderbolt upon the chambermaid.' One notes 'his
room'. There were no thunderbolts from the bisexual lord coming Polidori's way that night.

Finding a role for women has always been a problem for
those adapting *Frankenstein*. Mary Shelley gives them practi-
cally nothing to work on. *Dracula*, drawing on Polidori, opened
the way to *Buffy the Vampire Slayer* and TV 'undead' or walking
dead serials with high erotic content.

Frankenstein may have won the competition in June 1816.
But *The Vampyre* offered more to an increasingly permissive
culture wanting sexual interest as well as shudders. Us, in
other words. Dracula versus Frankenstein? The bloodsucker,
not the strangler, is currently marginally ahead.

What was Percy's contribution?

୬ଟ

Everything, some say. Camille Paglia, the fiery cross-grained feminist, said it loudest in reviewing *The Man Who Wrote Frankenstein* (2007) by the queer theorist and contrarian John Lauritsen. His thesis is proclaimed in his title. Percy, we are to understand, wrote the book, and its covert theme, hidden under Mary's authorship, is male-on-male love. As Paglia thundered:

> Lauritsen's book is important not only for its audacious theme but for the devastating portrait it draws of the insularity and turgidity of the current academy. As an independent scholar, Lauritsen is beholden to no one. As a consequence, he can fight openly with myopic professors and, without fear of retribution, condemn them for their inability to read and reason.

'Myopic' is ill-chosen. Those who, like Anne K. Mellor, have scrupulously examined Mary Shelley's literary remains (fully available only since 2004) note that up to 5,000 changes were made by Percy to Mary's (their?) manuscript – as many as six a page. They're not easily detected, even in the manuscript.

Touchingly, Mary had altered her handwriting to resemble Percy's. One can read submission into that. Mellor wouldn't agree.

In a legal sense Percy did, in 1818, 'own' the book. As with Jane Austen, contracts needed to be signed by a male hand. There was no author other than 'The Author' mentioned on the title and half-title pages but the first preface, in the 1818 edition, was manifestly by Percy – and, as even a cursory reading suggests, implies that there was a male author:

> I have thus endeavoured to preserve the truth of the elementary principles of human nature, while I have not scrupled to innovate upon their combinations. *The Iliad*, the tragic poetry of Greece, – Shakespeare, in *The Tempest* and *Midsummer Night's Dream*, – and most especially Milton, in *Paradise Lost*, conform to this rule; and the most humble novelist, who seeks to confer or receive amusement **from his labours**, may, without presumption, apply to prose fiction a licence, or rather a rule, from the adoption of which so many exquisite combinations of human feeling have resulted in the highest specimens of poetry. [my emphasis]

'His labours'? There are nine uses of 'I' in the short preface. It masculinises, buttressed by the lordly sweep of literary (the *Iliad* etc) references which, the uninformed reader would assume, only a public school and university education could furnish – to privileged males.

Mellor, censoriously, notes that the bulk of Percy's changes fall into one spoiling category:

> He typically changed her simple, Anglo-Saxon diction and straightforward or colloquial sentence structures into their more refined, complex, and Latinate equivalents. He is thus in large part responsible for the stilted, ornate, putatively Ciceronian prose style about which many readers have complained.

For 'Ciceronian' read 'male pomposity'.

Mellor lists chapter and verse examples of what she is talking about:

> When Frankenstein swore that he would 'not die until my adversary lay at my feet,' Percy rhetorically proclaimed that he would 'not relax the impending conflict until my own life, or that of my adversary, were extinguished'.

One change has, however, been universally conceded good by those who have pondered the known Percy input. When the Creature lunges, homicidally, towards Victor's throat, Percy changed 'fangs' to 'fingers'. That was well done. As his criminal record testifies, the Creature is a strangler, not a vampire. Leave that to John Polidori.

Mellor's disparagement convinces. Percy's was, if anything, a spoiling hand. But two things call for attention. Mary did not resist the stylistic spoiling, or insist on preserving her 'straightforward' female expression. How many earlier, spoken instructions did she acquiesce to?

Secondly, one must note that the manuscript Mellor scrutinises is a final draft: copy-text, the end of a long process of composition. One has no way of knowing what passed between the couple conversationally, unrecorded or in lost early drafts. Nor do we know what her audience suggested when she read out her spine-chiller to the assembled company at Villa Diodati. What we do know, from Mary Shelley's later remarks, is that the Ur-*Frankenstein* began at the point, a few chapters into the printed edition, where Victor describes the 'dreary November night'.

One change Percy made Mellor grants to have been structurally useful: 'He introduced all the references to Victor Frankenstein as the "author" of the creature.' In passages such as the following, for example:

> Remorse extinguished every hope [writes Victor]. I had been the author of unalterable evils, and I lived in daily fear lest the monster whom I had created should perpetrate some new wickedness.

Or this:

> 'Why do you call to my remembrance,' I rejoined [Victor is talking to his Creature], 'circumstances of which I shudder to reflect, that I have been the

> miserable origin and author? Cursed be the day, abhorred devil, in which you first saw light!'

Here Percy Shelley's hand was anything but spoiling. He was, among much else, a literary critic (viz. his *Defence of Poetry*) and an avowed neo-Platonist. By the judicious intrusion of the word 'author' in preference to, say, 'maker' or 'creator' (with their echoes of the Lord Almighty) he was giving his wife's book deeper sonority. By making this one verbal change, Percy invoked the Platonic/Aristotelian quarrel. Did poets (authors) create archetypal primary reality? Aristotle's rejoinder was that art, literature and performed drama (tragedy principally) were limited to mimesis, secondary reality. Imitation. Art is not made, but composed: it is not, in the case of tragedy (Aristotle's main interest in the surviving partial text of *The Poetics*), 'formed', but 'performed'.

That art was mimetically 'limited' by its necessary intermediation (it could imitate, but not primally create) was the argument of Gotthold Lessing's treatise *Laokoon*, inspired by his contemplation of statuary in the Vatican and reading Sophocles.

Lessing's text was published, in German, in 1766 and would still have been a topic of heated aesthetic discussion among the students at Ingolstadt in the early 1790s when Victor Frankenstein was there. *Laokoon* was not available in English until the 1830s. Percy would have had difficulty with Lessing's dense German but he quite possibly picked up second hand what Lessing was on about. Namely that by using its instrumentalities – pen and paper, chisel, hammer and marble, paint and canvas – art (and, in the broadest sense, the 'author') does not 'make'; it approximates to reality by imitation. Art and literature engage with reality, they do not achieve it.

This leads on to the large question hovering over *Frankenstein*. Is the Creature the imitation of a human being, quilted out of discarded parts? Or is it (he) something 'real' and original? A new, superhuman species? Or, as might have been thought in 1871, after Darwin's *The Descent of Man*, an evolutionary jump, leaving *Homo sapiens* in the same heap of the discarded as the Neanderthals?

This last would go some way to making sense of two of the many narrative cruxes in *Frankenstein*. Why, after making his two creatures, is Victor so appalled? So appalled, in fact, that he wants immediately to destroy them? Wanting that so much that he is prepared to destroy himself in the effort to unmake what he made?

Returning to what Percy loaded into the novel with the term 'author', an explanation suggests itself. It is clear at the outset that Victor intends to make a superior humanity, not superhumanity. A man who is marginally larger (two feet), stronger, and more agile; who can live in icy regions and scale mountains more nimbly than any Alpinist. Who can swim like a seal. This improved humanity will have a superior brain – the first Creature educates itself, reading Goethe and Milton, by the age of two. It will live on a 'rational' vegan diet of roots and berries. No animal need die for humanity. But, despite all improvement, still a man.

But when he looks at what he has made, Victor realises that he has not made a superior imitation of himself, he has bred a new species, a superhuman. What terrifies Victor, at the moment of his creatures' births, we may suppose, is that he has created something that could destroy him and his kind. To reverse James Whale's famous Frankenstein shout, 'It must not live! It must not live!'

Why 'The Modern Prometheus'?

☙

Following on from the above discussion of Percy's contribution to *Frankenstein*, it is interesting to consider the novel's subtitle: 'The Modern Prometheus'. Percy was, over the two years Mary was composing her novel for the publisher, meditating his epic drama *Prometheus Unbound*. The couple must, surely, have discussed their works in progress between themselves.

'The Modern Prometheus' is routinely invoked as what Frankenstein, at its thematic level, is concerned about – mankind's acquisition of technology which may either advance the species or ultimately destroy it. But other than the title page there is no reference to Titans, or things Promethean, in the text. References to *Paradise Lost*, Genesis and *The Sorrows of Young Werther* can be found on any number of pages.

Despite his rebellions against it, Percy Shelley received an excellent English education with a stress on classics (an interest in a career in surgery – cutting human meat – was brief, as it had been for Keats). Percy's knowledge of ancient Greek was particularly impressive. He quotes it promiscuously in his work. He did an admired translation of Plato's *Symposium* (its sexual heterodoxy was evidently much to his taste) and was prime among the early 19th-century classicists who had enthusiastically rediscovered Aeschylus. Little survives, in any entirety, of that Greek dramatist's tragedies other than *Prometheus Bound* and scraps, or foretellings, of the other two works in the lost trilogy, *Prometheus Unbound* and *Prometheus the Firegiver*.

The title of the last summarises Prometheus's role in mythology. Defying Zeus, jealously determined to keep all power to himself, Prometheus, the myth has it, gave the technology of fire (in the course of time, firepower) to humankind, for whom he had an affection (not a widespread thing in the Greek pantheon).

After Prometheus's theft, the Titans were overthrown and a furious Zeus chained the people-lover Prometheus to a mountain in the Caucasus to be tormented by an eagle which every night devoured his liver. Since he was still a god, it was renewed every morning. He is rescued by Hercules in myth, and in Shelley's poem by his moral growth as he suffers on the crags.

Percy Shelley was fascinated by Prometheus and was proficient enough in ancient Greek to work out his fascination in a major work of literature. Mary Godwin was a brilliant and well-read young woman when she fell in love with Shelley. A credit to her father, who superintended her home schooling. But she knew little Greek. Her Greek deficit was soon a matter of concern between her and Percy. In 1814 she confessed herself flummoxed by a line in Greek he quoted from Aeschylus' *Prometheus Bound*. In her journal that week she resolved to teach herself ancient Greek. But her life, over the next four years (scandal, children, exile, disowned by father, travel), was so hectic that her good resolution foundered. It was 1820 before she at last renewed her Greek studies. But by that time *Frankenstein* had been published.

Why, then, did Mary subtitle her work 'The Modern Prometheus'? My belief is that she didn't. It was Percy, then obsessed with *Prometheus*, who inserted it – as he also inserted the explanatory preface to the 1818 edition, intimating his co-authorship of *Frankenstein*.

If it were his doing, 'The Modern Prometheus' was a mistake. It's a titular signpost pointing in the wrong direction, leading the reader up wrong paths. Who, if one regards the text, is the modern Prometheus? Routinely the answer is Victor Frankenstein. But it doesn't fit. Victor doesn't give new technology to mankind as does Prometheus. He resolutely denies mankind the benefit of his discovery.

Victor Frankenstein is no Titan; that is, no giant possessed of superhuman strength and capacity for suffering. He is frail, physically weak, forever prone to fainting fits and for a good quarter of the novel bedridden. No need to chain him to a mountainside. The giant, with superhuman (godly) powers is the Creature. He is frequently on the sheer face of mountains. Tormented (if not by eagles) and titanic.

'The Modern Prometheus' is a misnomer, perpetrated against the grain of Mary's narrative, by her husband. 'A Modern Adam' would have fit the novel, as Mary wrote it, better.

What did Mary Shelley earn?

❧

A beginning authoress in the early to mid-19th century often found it helpful to use a male front to get into print. Anonymity, or gender neutrality, has always been one way of doing it: from George Eliot to J.K. Rowling. Help from a friendly male intermediary was another means of getting publishers to take notice.

Pride and Prejudice, whose author is pictured on the tenners in my pocket, had her 'First Impressions' (then so-called) sent by her father, George, to Cadell, a publisher thought to be favourable to women writers.

Not this woman. The Revd Austen's letter came back, scrawled across it, woundingly, 'declined by return of post'. The novel, now regarded as one of the greatest in English fiction, waited sixteen years to see the light of print. Parts of it (notably the 1790s war fear and militia mobilisation) were dusty on publication. We would probably have had more than six novels from Austen had Cadell not let her know, in her authorial youth, that she was useless.

Frankenstein, once written up in late 1817, was touted round London publishers by Percy, with the covering letter that he was acting 'for a friend abroad'.* Gender unknown, but

* Percy and Mary were by now married. Married women had particular problems signing contracts or owning literary property at this time.

male implied. John Murray, Byron's publisher, was not interested. Percy then turned to his own publisher Charles Ollier who took only three days to reject *Frankenstein*.*

Since there was nothing to indicate the gender of the author it would be assumed by the reading public to be a male. (Ollier probably knew it wasn't – or not entirely.) The preface (written by Percy) audibly rang with a male voice. Through and through masculinity was further confirmed by there being no woman one could call heroine in the narrative.

The onion-layered narrative of the novel has three narrators: all male (assuming that's what the Creature can be called). Thomas Carlyle was the first of many early readers to assume the work was by 'Godwin's son-in-law'. It was also, Carlyle guessed before reading it, 'another unnatural disgusting fiction'.

Why, though, did Murray and Ollier and possibly other houses so roundly reject *Frankenstein*? Most likely because the slightest whiff of blasphemous, atheistical and Godwinian ideas scared the average library reader. *Frankenstein* seemed to be an apologia for violent crime. Why? Because as Percy Shelley put it elsewhere, following Godwin, 'treat a person ill and they will become wicked'. The Creature is treated ill; he becomes wicked.

....

* Here and throughout this entry I am dependent on William St Clair's account of the publication of Frankenstein in *The Reading Nation in the Romantic Period* (2004).

One scene described by the Creature to Frankenstein makes the point. On leaving the woods for good in midsummer the Creature had found himself by:

> a deep and rapid river ... I heard the sound of voices, that induced me to conceal myself under the shade of a cypress. I was scarcely hid, when a young girl came running towards the spot where I was concealed, laughing as if she ran from some one in sport. She continued her course along the precipitous sides of the river, when suddenly her foot slipt, and she fell into the rapid stream. I rushed from my hiding place, and, with extreme labour from the force of the current, saved her, and dragged her to shore. She was senseless; and I endeavoured, by every means in my power, to restore animation, when I was suddenly interrupted by the approach of a rustic, who was probably the person from whom she had playfully fled. On seeing me, he darted towards me, and, tearing the girl from my arms, hastened towards the deeper parts of the wood. I followed speedily, I hardly knew why; but when the man saw me draw near, he aimed a gun, which he carried, at my body, and fired. I sunk to the ground, and my injurer, with increased swiftness, escaped into the wood.

One has a certain sympathy with the unknown peasant. He comes upon an ill-clad giant vigorously rubbing the body of his unconscious daughter. What father wouldn't at least draw his gun?

The next child he meets, Victor's little brother William, the Creature strangles. His killing spree has begun. Understanding why criminals commit crime was of no interest to the authorities. It rarely is. The Godwins, father and daughter and son-in-law, were preaching to the wind.

Eventually the orphaned *Frankenstein* was taken by a publisher of last resort, Lackington, a culturally indiscriminate mass producer. They did, by way of consolation, have a line of supernatural fiction: most interestingly Sarah Utterson's *Tales of the Dead* (1813), the English translation of Jean-Baptiste Benôit Eyriès's *Fantasmagoriana*, the volume of (originally German) ghost stories which had started the whole thing off at Villa Diodati. Only Mary and Percy would have made the connection.

Lackington did not value their acquisition. *Frankenstein's* early career would resemble that of an unexploded bomb, waiting fifteen years or more for detonation.

A short one-volume publication would have suited the novel best. The volume I am using, for example, is some 155 pages. Lackington's *Frankenstein* was, by contrast, inflated – by large print, gappy leading, and unnecessary white spaces – into a three-decker for the library market. The novel was allowed a modest print run of 500.* The author was given

---

* The recent auction of Byron's presentation copy sold for half a million dollars. The inscription by Mary makes no reference to Villa Diodati.

a basic profit-sharing contract yielding the Shelleys a third of revenue after costs. The novel came out on New Year's Day 1818, costing for libraries a heavily discounted ten shillings or so. The posted price was sixteen shillings and sixpence. Things went from bad to worse. The delivery and advertising of the book were bungled. The edition sold badly, yielding the Shelleys little or nothing. There was no encouragement for Mary Shelley to continue as a novelist.

A breakthrough came in 1831, with the Colburn and Bentley Standard Novel edition (see page 100). For the copyright and the introduction Mary Shelley received £30. It was, as William St Clair bleakly records, 'the last financial benefit she or her family were ever to receive'. For 200 years the British reading public has received, from Mary Shelley, a lot more.

Appendix:
Frankenstein Digested

by John Crace

John Crace is the parliamentary sketch writer for the
Guardian *newspaper, for which he also writes the*
regular 'Digested Read' feature. His many books include
I, Maybot: The Rise and Fall *and, with John Sutherland,*
the multi-volume The Incomplete Shakespeare.

St Petersburg, March 17

My dear Sister,

Forgive me for including so much in this letter about our early lives that you will already know, but Mary Shelley is but eighteen years old and this is her first novel and she has little experience in beginning such an undertaking. Save to say that the effusions that so entranced my soul as a child have taken me in search of the Pole and it was while we were sailing north that we did espy a man gigantic in stature bound across the ice. Some two hours later we did encounter another man in a piteous state, close to death, whom we took on board.

'Unhappy man,' he cried. 'Do you share my madness?' This is the story he told us.

Affectionately yours, Robert Walton.

Book One

I am by birth a Genevese, my family one of the most distinguished in the republic. Though not one whose name, Frankenstein, is known by anyone living there. For many years I was the only child, until some years later my parents were out walking and did acquire a girl named Elizabeth who became my cousin. At some point or other, my parents also had a second son.

While growing up, my closest friend was Henry Clerval, the son of a merchant, and for many seasons did we argue over the philosophical works of Cornelius Agrippa, until one night there was such an electrical storm – such as might have been heard by Mary Shelley on her vacation with Byron in the French Alps – that I decided to devote my life to science. A little while later, my mother died, her last words begging me to marry Elizabeth. Something I was curiously reluctant to do, possibly because I was more attracted to Henry.

While studying at the University of Ingolstadt, I succeeded in finding the cause of the generation of life, a discovery that so astonished me, I completely forgot how I had done it and so was forced to start again. Working day and night over many months, I collected bones and body parts from charnel houses and created a being eight feet in length. It was only when I had finished my monster that I noticed his skin and eyes had turned yellow and so alarmed was I when he attempted to speak to me that I ran out into the street where I bumped into Clerval. I later returned to the house to discover that the Monster had fled, but couldn't be bothered to wonder where it might have gone and instead lapsed into a bout of intense hypochondria.

Upon my recovery two years later, I received a letter from Elizabeth informing me that my parents had acquired a nanny, Justine, whom they had also found out walking, and reminding me that my younger brother who had never previously been named was called William. By coincidence, the following day my father also sent me a letter saying that William had been brutally murdered and that Justine was the prime suspect.

That evening, there was a flash of light and I did espy the monster, about whom I had totally forgotten, at the window and immediately realised it was the Daemon who had murdered William. I rushed home, prepared to unmask the Monster as the killer, but fearing my accusation would be dismissed as the rantings of a madman and that Justine would not be exculpated, I decided it was better if she were convicted and executed. For reasons best known to herself, Justine then confessed and my hypochondria kicked in again. No one had ever been as miserable as me. Apart from Justine, possibly.

Book Two

Geneva had become disagreeable to me – our house was one of misery – so I moved to Belrive, determined to extinguish the life of the creature. Out walking among the mountains near Chamonix I came across the wretch.

'Devil be gone,' I cried.

'Hear my life,' the abhorred monster replied.

This is what he told me.

'Finding some XXXXXL clothes and a pair of size 23 shoes fortunately lying around your bedroom, I fled your house and ran to lose myself in the countryside. There I survived by eating berries and amused myself by learning at least three languages – German, French and English – that were to stand me in good stead later. For shelter, I hid in the barn of a hovel occupied by an old man, his daughter Agatha and his son Felix, who was in love with a Turkish woman, named Safie.

'"Oh my Arabian beauty," he would swoon.

'"I'm Turkish," she would reply.

'"Oh my Arabian beauty," he would swoon again.

'After several months, I plucked up the courage to enter their hovel, believing they might befriend me. At first all went well, as the old man was blind, but when the others returned they fled in terror at the sight of my hideousness. I escaped into the night, determined to return to Geneva to take my revenge on you, my creator, by killing the brother you had never really cared about and framing Justine for his murder.

'What torment I felt! Too hideous for any woman to have sex with. The archetypal involuntary celibate. So I set out to track you down and beg you to create an eight foot woman to be my one true love.

'Create a female for me,' the Daemon implored me. 'And we will disappear together to South America – though I know not where that is or how the hell we're going to get there without anyone noticing us – where we will bother Man no more.'

Initially I refused the vile incel but upon hearing his entreaties I compassionated him and promised to deliver him of a female companion.

'Know that I shall follow you wherever you go,' the Daemon warned, before descending the mountain faster than an eagle.

Book Three

My father was pressing me to marry Elizabeth, but I determined that I was happier travelling to England with my dear friend Clerval. First we visited London, that wonderful and celebrated city, before heading out on the A4 to travel to Windsor. From there we went west to Newbury, thence up to Oxford via the A34, before passing through Matlock en route to Edinburgh. There we parted company, and I travelled alone north to the Orkneys, there to create the companion for the incel.

For many days and nights did I travail over my new creature. Nearly were my labours complete when I did see the Daemon at the casement – he spent a lot of time hanging around outside windows – and upon that moment I did regret my decision and tore my female creature limb from limb.

'You will regret being so cruel to thy incel,' the Monster shrieked. 'I shall be with you on your wedding night.'

The following morning I received a letter from Henry, inviting me to join him in Perth. I set aside my vile instruments and set forth in a skiff, only to find I had managed to sail around the northern tip of Scotland and land in Ireland in about four hours flat. Upon arrival, I found myself accused of the murder of a man whose body had been found only hours earlier lying in the mud. I fell back comatose when I learned that the victim was Clerval, who had mysteriously anticipated me getting lost en route to Perth and come to Ireland himself, and for many days I hovered between life and death in another state of extreme hypochondria.

Upon my recovering some many weeks later, it was determined that I wasn't the murderer after all as I had been in the Orkneys when the foul deed was done and my father came to take me back to Geneva. During our journey home, I told my father everything. How my monster had killed William and Henry.

'A thousand times would I have shed my own blood, drop by drop, rather than they had died,' I wept, yet again failing to take any responsibility for my own actions, for I could quite easily have saved them both.

In Paris, I received a letter from Elizabeth, reminding me it had been my mother's wish that we should get married and that she was getting a bit tired of hanging around waiting. With Henry dead, I could see no reason to delay the matter further and so on my return we duly did the paperwork. On our wedding night, while I was busy downstairs worrying about one of my minor ailments, I heard a scream from the bedroom. I ran upstairs to find Elizabeth lying strangled and the Daemon standing over her body, exclaiming a loud and fiendish laugh.

Moments later, my father also dropped down dead and tears streamed from my eyes. I vowed to hunt the daemon down like a chamois and would not rest until he was dead. And so I have chased him ever further north, across the frozen wastelands and thus it was that you found me at death's door.

Walton (in continuation)

My dear sister,

Will I ever see England again? It seems I might as I have decided to give up my quest and head south again. For once, Frankenstein's health concerns turned out to be genuine and he died in my arms on board my ship. As he lay dying, the Daemon appeared at the window.

'My agony was superior to thine,' he said competitively. 'Farewell Frankenstein. Now I too shall die.' And with that he jumped overboard.

Splash.

Is Heathcliff a Murderer?

In this new edition of his bestselling classic, literary sleuth John Sutherland regales fans of nineteenth-century fiction with the anomalies and conundrums that have emerged from his years of close reading and good-natured pedantry.

Is Oliver Twist dreaming? Why does Dracula come to England? Does Becky kill Jos in *Vanity Fair*? How does Frankenstein make his monsters? And, of course: is Heathcliff really a murderer?

ISBN: 9781785782992 (paperback) / 9781785783005 (ebook)

Can Jane Eyre Be Happy?

In this follow-up to the enormously successful *Is Heathcliff a Murderer?*, John Sutherland plays literary detective and investigates tantalising conundrums from Daniel Defoe to Virginia Woolf.

How does Magwitch swim to shore with a 'great iron' on his leg? Where does Fanny Hill keep her contraceptives? Does Clarissa Dalloway have an invisible taxi? And, of course: can Jane Eyre really be happy?

ISBN: 9781785783012 (paperback) / 9781785783029 (ebook)